There is no greater agony
than bearing an untold story inside you.
—Maya Angelou

❧

This is my story.

LIFE'S UNCERTAIN JOURNEY

One Woman's Battle for Her Sanity, Her Marriage and Her Family

G. Nadine Davis

Charlotte, NC
www.metanoialifepublishing.com

G. Nadine Davis © 2018
ISBN No. 9780999830802
ISBN: 0999830805
Library of Congress Control Number: 2018900725
Metanoia Publishing, Charlotte, NC

Cover Art by Donald U. Palmer II

Disclaimer Clause
The author has made every effort to ensure the accuracy of the information within this book was correct at time of publication. The author does not assume and hereby disclaims any liability to any part for any loss, damage, or disruption caused by errors or omissions, whether such errors or omissions result from accident, negligence, or any other cause.

Different Bible versions were used throughout this book. I do not prefer one bible version over another. This will assist the readers in the translation of scripture that they may not be familiar with.

This book is dedicated to all women who feel that there is no hope for their current situation. My desire is to help them avoid the turmoil and tragedies I suffered and provide them with hope. His name is Jesus!

Different Bible versions were used throughout this book. I do not prefer one Bible version over another. This will assist the readers in the translation of scripture that they may not be familiar with.

CONTENTS

ACKNOWLEDGMENTS

To God be all the glory for the great things He has done on behalf of the children of men.

I am grateful to so many who stood with me and encouraged me along this awesome journey. I thank God for my husband, John, who has made my life such a joy! To see how God honored His promise to deliver him still brings tears to my eyes.

To my children, especially by daughters and granddaughters, I leave this legacy. I thank God for you. I watched my daughter, Kimberly, as she followed in my footsteps, yielding her life for the Master's use through some pretty tough times of her own. My granddaughters also have linked up with the King of kings and Lord of lords as very young ladies. I can't wait to see how God uses them. My sons are all real men! I say that because they came through the turmoil of my ignorance as a young mother unscathed, strong, successful, wonderful providers for their families and mighty men of valor, who love God and bring me great honor.

I cannot say enough about Jan and Brenda, my compadres in faith who embraced me when I moved to Charlotte and have never stopped loving and encouraging me. Then there is Joy and all my beloved prayer warrior sisters at Moms in Prayer International. What an excellent expression of faith and commitment to prayer these women are. I thank God for this powerful ministry that helped pray my babies out of some real, troubling situations.

Finally, I thank God for Pastor Kelvin Smith, whose love for God and His people overflows in a congregation that represents well what heaven will be like—every nation, kindred, and tongue united in praise and worship to the One True God. He prayed for and trusted the work God was doing in my life, which really was a blessing to me.

PREFACE

*The Spirit of the Sovereign Lord is on me, because the
Lord has anointed me to proclaim good news to the poor.
He has sent me to bind up the brokenhearted, to proclaim
freedom for the captives and release from darkness for the
prisoners,[a] to proclaim the year of the Lord's favor and
the day of vengeance of our God, to comfort all who mourn,
and provide for those who grieve in Zion—to bestow on
them a crown of beauty instead of ashes, the oil of joy
instead of mourning, and a garment of praise instead of a
spirit of despair. They will be called oaks of righteousness,
a planting of the Lord for the display of his splendor.*

—Isaiah 61:1–3 NLT

I am writing this book with the expressed desire of leaving a legacy
of faith and trust in God, His Word, and His ability to do exceed-
ingly, abundantly above all that we can ask or think. I desire that
my daughters, granddaughters, spiritual daughters, and ultimately
every person who reads this book will come to know that God is not
only very real but that He loves and cares for them more than they
can imagine. I pray that you too come to know that you are not in
this world without hope. God is not thinking your life up as it goes

along. No, He has a distinct plan and purpose for your life. I pray that you will learn what that purpose is and then trust exclusively in Jesus Christ, the son of the Living God to make it all happen!

Today, we live in a culture that has totally forgotten about God. People enter into their daily routines totally oblivious to His presence and divine providence over their meager lives (Matt. 5:4). We have no idea that we are in the last days, and that sooner than we think, God's judgment is coming upon all who do not believe in His Son whom He sent to save us from that judgment (John 3:18)!

Father God, I ask You to move upon the heart of this reader by your Holy Spirit. Cause their eyes to be opened so that they may see and their ears to be unstopped so that they can hear and know just how much you love them. Help me to share how You pursued and came after me, how You found me and revealed Yourself and Your Son to me. Help me to explain how You opened my eyes to Your unfailing Truth, rescued me from Satan's plot to trick me out of the life you had prepared for me, for my husband, and for my children. Help them to realize that Satan and his band of demons are very real and that they plot every single day to trick us with lies so that we will wind up in hell to forever in torment and serving him. May they see how, in spite of my ignorance, You came after me, forgave me for my ignorant and sinful actions, and then empowered me to live for You and fight for my family. Turn their heart toward You, Father, so that they too may be found by You and rescued from Satan's plot to steal, kill, destroy, and keep them from the abundant life you have for them (John 10:10).

So beloved, as you read of the incidents that took place in my walk of faith, keep your heart open to hear the voice of the Father calling to you. He says, "…Today if you will hear His voice, do not harden your hearts…" (Hebrews 3:15 KJV).

INTRODUCTION

This is the real-life story of how Jesus Christ revealed Himself to me and set me free from a life that was filled with great turmoil and much darkness. I was a lewd woman, an unfaithful wife, and a neglectful mother. Demons ruled me, and Satan shackled my mind and kept it in a horrible state of depression. This journey that God brought me through began with very disappointing circumstances. This journey tells the story of how I grew up with a powerful and distinct loathing in my heart for God and anything that represented Him. I was totally unaware that every situation and problem that had taken place in my life was specifically designed to keep me from God. With each and every issue that arose in my life, I was being provided convincing evidence to support my theory that there is no God!

I want to tell a little about my journey because I believe there are countless others on the same journey and have no idea where it's going to lead. It is my prayer that my testimony serves as hope and encouragement to anyone reading this book today that God is real, He loves you very much and truly desires to help you—if you will only believe it.

You will read about how my diminished mental stability and raging rebellion against God led to my association with demonic forces that I didn't believe existed. Demons that crept their way into my life with each disappointing circumstance I encountered. They snuck in without me even knowing it. They were too strong for me to conquer alone and too subtle for me to even detect. There were so many terrible situations and incidents that were so strong they caused me to seek the silence and solitude of death itself. Thoughts of committing suicide became the only possibility out of the pain and torment I was in. I am also sharing my story because the Lord allowed me to live to tell it! He did not allow the enemy of my soul to triumph over me. I am alive today because He loved me and had mercy on me. This is my story of how God came after me and revealed Himself to me, all in answer to my mother's prayers.

I am an old lady today with so very much to be thankful for. I say, just as the older women would sing in that old gospel song, "If it had not been for the Lord on my side, where would I be?" May my testimony encourage and provide you with evidence and the hope that your journey is not yet over. May it awaken you to just how powerful God is and how He can take your impossible situation and work it out for your good. He loves you and wants you to know it!

This is my testimony. It is the testimony of how God pursued me and revealed to me that not only was He real but that He truly loved me. He also revealed the real enemy of my life, whose plot was to steal, kill and destroy not only me but my family and our future. This enemy tricked me three times into attempting suicide at his bequest. He taunted me with his lies that nobody cared about or loved me. They were all lies—lies designed to rob me of the plan and destiny my heavenly Father had planned for me. Today, I still get angry when I think about it. I now know that had the Lord not stepped in to help me, I would not have lived to witness His redemptive power and the wonderful "new life" He had waiting for me and my family. I would have not known the eleven precious grandchildren the Lord would ultimately bless me with. My children would have been showing them photographs of a grandmother they would never come to know. I also would not have lived to see God change and transform my husband into a loving and passionate man of God. I would have missed it all because of a liar. Believe me when I say that I get angry about what could have happened and know that it is directed at the right person. It is truly painful to watch as others fall prey to his lies. As scripture tells us, our battle is not with flesh and blood. Our only true enemy is Satan.

I am telling my story to warn people that the same old diabolical plot of lies has been playing out since the beginning of time. Satan has no new tricks. They are the same ones he used in the Garden of Eden when man and woman first showed up. The sad part is that so many people are not paying any attention to this liar. They are instead blaming family, bosses, friends, you name it. We don't seem to get the fact that the battle we wage is not against flesh and blood. I pray my story helps others to understand this and begin to put the blame where it truly lies, at Satan's feet. We need not be tricked by him any longer. I pray that my story will help you to see his plot of lies and the truth he'd rather you not know—that God is real and He loves you very much. He wants to help you to get loose from the chain of lies so you can walk in victory. He sent His Son, who was born of a woman. God's Son was born of a woman! He came with the specific mission to destroy the works of Satan. He now offers freedom to everyone that will listen to Him and believe Him. He wants to give us a life that is both abundant and eternal! The enemy hasn't gone away just yet. However, his lies will no longer be able to trick us into thinking that there is no hope or remedy for our life's situations.

My life story is not fiction. It actually happened, and I have friends and family, including my children, who can bear witness to it. They remember the woman I was and the transformed woman God is creating. I say "is creating" because God's work in me is not finished. I don't want you to misinterpret what I'm telling you. As the apostle Paul would say, I have not fully apprehended all that the Lord has for me, but I press on to perfection and maturity that only He can provide.

I pray also that this testimony will leave a legacy of faith in God and of how the power of prayer can change the trajectory of anyone's life! It is my prayer that long after the Lord has called me home, my daughters and sons, granddaughters and grandsons, and spiritual daughters and sons will remember my story and testimony that God is real and He does have a plan and a purpose for their lives! The same miracles He did for me and my husband He will do for them. Don't just take my word for it. Begin searching for Him yourself. It starts with a simple conversation, such as, "Lord, I don't know you. Please reveal Yourself and Your Son, Jesus Christ, to me. I realize that I've lived my life ignorant of who you really are. Please help me!" Not only is He listening—He promises that you will find Him.

Jeremiah 29:11–14a in the Amplified Bible says: "For I know the plans and thoughts that I have for you, says the Lord, plans for peace and well-being and not for disaster to give you a future and a hope. Then, you will call on me and you will come and pray to me and I will hear (your voice) and I will listen to you. Then with (deep longing) you will seek me and require me (as a vital necessity) and (you will) find me when you search for me with all your heart. I will be found by you…"

1

GOD WAS NOT MY FRIEND

In the beginning God created the heavens and the earth. The earth was formless and empty, and darkness covered the deep waters...

—Gen. 1:1–2a (NLT)

As a young woman growing up, I was oblivious to the Love that God had for me. My young life started off with such tragedy that there was no way for me to deduce that the Love of God was even present. My parents moved to Washington, DC, from Alabama when I was very young. I remember my mom stayed home with my brother and I while my dad worked. Sometimes he would come home smelling awful with some dead animal over his shoulder that I later realized was roadkill. My dad was an awesome cook, so I never knew what the meat was, but it sure was good. I also remember my mom had a beautiful voice and sang at church. She was also a praying woman. However, one of the things I remember most was their fighting. I remember pulling at my dad's leg trying to make him stop hitting my mom. I don't recall the reason for their fights. I just remember the beatings my mom took. He would hit her so hard. Sometime later my mom became very sick. We were living with one of my father's sisters at the time. My mom was taken to the hospital but stayed there for what seemed a very long time. When she finally did come home, she was bedbound. She looked sicker when she came home than when she left. I remember one day my mom called me and my little brother into her room. She told us she loved us so very much and that she was going to see us again in God's kingdom. At our young age, we didn't really understand what she meant. However, today I understand totally!

The day came when the ambulance came for my mom. I can't remember how long she was gone, but I do remember that not long after she left, my dad came and picked me and my little brother up from school really early. When we got home, he told us that our mom would not be coming home. It had been my hope that she would be coming home soon. However, our dad told us that she had died. My dad and my little brother wept so hard. I just couldn't believe what he had just told us. I was so shocked I couldn't even cry. How could this be! How could a loving God let my mother die, leaving my younger brother and I without a mother? I tried to be strong for my little brother's sake. That would become an ongoing effort throughout my life—trying to "be strong" when I knew I hurt so badly. Suppressing those hurts would ultimately erupt into something ugly. Needless to say, I wondered and pondered over what was going to happen next. Our dad attempted to care for us, but his sister had determined that it would be better if she took care of us. So, there we were, being traumatized again. First our mom died and then we were being taken away from our dad, the only one we knew really loved us. So, you see how my young life was not off to a good start. Not at all!

As I grew up, I began to blame much of my heartache and pain on my aunt. I did not feel any love from her or her family mostly because of the anger and bitterness that had begun to set in on my heart. I just couldn't get over the bad turn of events in my life. But let me say in retrospect, God used this woman to introduce me to some culture and things I may not have ever learned or experienced. She paid for piano lessons that ultimately produced a fair piano player and a lively saxophone player in my teenage years. She also periodically would take my brother and me on trips and to visit our older step brother and sisters that lived in Alabama. I believe she did what she could for us, but even so I always felt that my brother and I were relegated to the leftovers. Some would have called us ungrateful, but they did not know our pain. Even after I became an adult, the aroma of my sad beginnings as a child still wafted through my nostrils, often making me sick in my mind. What did I ever do to deserve all this? It was very hard for me because I could never express my pain to anyone. Not only did I not know how to but no one seemed to want to hear it. As far as I was concerned, my little brother and I were left to this fate, and those who were supposed to care for us didn't do a good job at it. Nope. We had to look out for ourselves!

My mom knew Jesus. She told me about Him and how He loved me. However, that God that my momma said loved us so much gave her cancer and took her away from us. That didn't seem like love to me, and I didn't want any part of Him. Why would God allow two helpless babies to be left at the mercy of the world and in circumstances over which they had no power? No, I didn't like that God, and as far as I was concerned, He didn't like me either.

To many, my aunt was the image of Christianity. The noble deed of taking in these helpless children would truly go down in the annals of Christianity. However, I would learn that what went on at church and what happened behind closed doors could be quite different. We attended church loyally. I recall watching some church members dancing their little shouting jig all over folk's feet. They even slapped off a couple of hats here and there. But there were days during the week at home when there was gambling going on, drinking, and moonshine and home brew being made and sold, not to mention the cursing and the arguments. If this is what went on in Christian homes, then by my assessment, it was all fake and people were just hypocrites!

As I grew older, I became more bitter. I even recall one of the deacons who came to pick me up to go visit with his daughter. When we got there, she wasn't home. As a matter of fact, no one else was home. He had plans for me that I'm sure my aunt didn't know about. However, he was surprised by the unexpected arrival of his son, who I held on to for dear life. I begged him not to leave me alone and that I wanted to go home. He assured me his dad would take me, but I asked him to go with us. He seemed so puzzled, but I couldn't tell him what his dad had tried to do to me. When I did get home and told what had happened, I was told I brought it on myself. I must have done something but never was it mentioned that I had been treated badly by a deacon of the church. I tell you, it really helped to further harden my heart. I began to really resent my life. There was no one to protect me! Several times I attempted to run away only to be brought back to face my fate.

When I was just a teenager, I was coerced into marrying a young man I hardly knew. He had followed me home one day from my after-school job. When I told my aunt I really didn't know him, I don't think she believed me. I had started working when I was fourteen because I wanted to be able to buy nice things for my brother at Christmastime. My little brother never got what he really wanted for Christmas. I worked as a youth counselor at a church several blocks from where we lived. This job really made me feel as though there was some hope and I could get some things I wanted. Wrong! Guess who got my earnings? Yes…my aunt.

The church where I worked was often visited by neighborhood youth who would come play on their basketball courts. I would see this young boy playing basketball but never engaged in a conversation or anything with him. I had no idea that he was even interested in me. As a matter of fact, I was quite startled to catch a glimpse of him coming up our front steps behind me. I knew I didn't invite him to follow me home, and there he was, following me right up to my door. I think I cursed at him when I saw him. My uncle, who was sitting on the porch, called my aunt and told her that I was cursing. He made no mention of this strange young man that was behind me. Well, I suppose my aunt seemed to think he was a rather well-mannered young man, as he introduced himself. My aunt invited him in and would later attempt to convince me that he seemed to be an appropriate suitor for me. Well, I really was not into dating; however, he seemed to show up rather consistently at my aunt's house to see me. I didn't find him offensive or anything, but I had my heart set on going to college. My aunt had always made me feel inferior, and I wanted to prove to her that I was not only smart but wanted to become a lawyer. Yet, I was encouraged to allow him to visit with me. Then one day his mother shows up at our house, and I began to hear talks about marriage. I became concerned because I had already voiced my desire to go off to college to become a lawyer. As my aunt began to share the notion of marriage, I tried telling her that I didn't want to get married. However, she began to make it quite clear to me that if I thought she was going to take care of me after graduation, I was wrong. She suggested that I had allowed this young man to take advantage of me, and she wasn't going to have an unwed mother in her house. I was floored by this turn of events. Where in the world was all this coming from? Where was she getting this information from? Anyway—she strongly suggested that if this young man had an interest in me, I should consider him. She told me that the reality was that no one had the money to send me to college. My dad certainly didn't make enough money to afford a college education for me. She suggested I get real because after graduation I needed to be moving on. She attempted to soothe my pain and suggested that it wouldn't be all that bad because he would probably get drafted to go to Vietnam. Then I would get his soldier benefits as his wife. I was hoping my dad would object and not allow this to happen, but my aunt suggested that since I was dating this guy, there was a possibility I would come up pregnant—like my momma! Well, where did that come from? What in the world was she saying about my mom? That was a bit much for me to hear, and I strongly resented it. Now, I was really angry, but what was the use? I couldn't talk back, or I would get that familiar backhand. Once again I surmised that there wasn't much I could do. Then on one of my crying bouts, the thought came to mind that this just may be a ray of hope for me. If I married this guy, my marriage would mean leaving my aunt's house. I wouldn't have to live under her roof anymore. I began to relish the thought of moving away and being on my own. The only worry I had was for my little brother. But what could I do? Here again, my life was being shaped beyond my control.

Well, we were married when I was much too young to understand what marriage was. However, I couldn't wait for us to leave. He didn't seem all that bad of a guy. I didn't really get to know him well over our short courting period, but that would certainly change over time. All I wanted was out of my aunt's house.

Just before we would finally leave my aunt's house, I made a startling discovery. I recall a time when an insurance agent came to ask me questions because my husband wanted to take out an insurance policy. Well, the agent asked me if I had any medical problems, and I told him yes. I suffered terribly with asthma. However, for some strange reason, one of my cousins that was present at that time told the agent that I didn't have asthma. I would later learn that she was trying to help me because telling them this would possibly hinder my husband from getting coverage, but how was I to know that at sixteen? Well, when he found out about it, he hit me in the face for lying. Boy, my brother and younger cousin witnessed it and wanted to jump him, but he was much older than they were. I cried, and he cried too. He apologized to me profusely. Of course, I believed him. However, it is very true that if they hit you once, it will happen again…and it did. Suffice it to say that I had no idea I was married to someone with anger issues also. Like I said, I knew very little about what kind of person he was and had no idea what things he may have endured as a young child that would cause him to get so upset as to strike me.

Let me stop here because there is one thing I do not want to take place as I share my testimony. I don't want anyone to blame this man simply because I am the one telling the story. There are always two sides to every story. The fact was that neither of us knew anything about life, much less marriage. We were much too young to marry in the first place. I do not blame him for my past. God has done wonders in my heart and helped me to realize that he, like me, was in the devil's clutches. I truly believe he loved me and wanted to provide for me. He certainly didn't realize he was getting damaged goods. He didn't know my past, my pain, or my darkness when he asked to marry me. He is a wonderful man and father to my three older children.

For eleven years we tried to make things work. As I mentioned, we both had terrible anger issues that would often end in fighting. It seemed the things I saw happening with my mom and dad were now happening to me. I was always hoping that our marriage would get better. I also knew I had nowhere to go. I would rather face my chances with him than go back to my aunt's house.

As I stayed in the marriage, my heart just grew darker and colder. I began meeting people who would teach me new things. I learned how to smoke, how to drink, and yes, how to cheat. This all became part of my new life of freedom from my aunt. They were truly dark times. I recall my husband and I purchased a picture of Satan and hung it on our living-room wall. We thought it was cool. We had no idea who we invited into our home. I began smoking marijuana, taking drugs, and just cruising along without a care. One night I was so high that I watched Satan come down from the picture on the wall and talk with me. Those were some pretty powerful drugs! He promised me he would take good care of me, but he also warned me never to pray. He told me that if I ever prayed to God, He would strike me down dead because of the way I lived my life. So, guess what—I never prayed! That lie set me and my children up for some terrible times.

I would fall into years of hell-bound debauchery. I started doing unthinkable things to myself, endangering my children. Believe me; living in darkness is no joke. It has a stronghold over the mind that causes one to lose grip on reality. The more I lived in the darkness, the worse things became for me. Suffice it to say my marriage was rife with struggle, affairs, violence, and lies. I couldn't blame my husband. We were both in trouble. We were both under the influence of a terrible taskmaster called Satan. He had it out for the both of us from the very beginning.

As I said earlier, I was no angel. I became a very wicked woman. I'm sure he can recall some very unsavory things about me that I don't even remember. However, I do want you to know that beauty came out of all the turmoil and despair, three precious gems that we both love dearly. After our divorce, I never wanted my children to resent or think badly toward their father. We both took them through hell, yet they love and respect both of us. I tell you...when I look at the adults they have become, by the grace of God, I know there is hope for everyone who will believe it! Our children suffered great trauma, the kind that could cripple their lives. However, the Lord had mercy on them and kept them through it all! Glory to His name! I often tell moms today the importance of them praying for their children. I didn't pray for mine during those horrible times of darkness because of Satan's lie. However I believe they were spared because of my mother's prayers for me.

You may have heard that saying that hurt people hurt people. It is so very true. The circumstances that followed me left me cold, bitter, angry, and just plain nasty. I can't even count the number of times I disrespected and dishonored my ex-husband. Remember, no one taught me how to be a wife or a mother, and I did poorly at both. We would encounter many a trauma over our marriage. One such trauma was the shooting of my baby brother. After one of our brutal fights, my husband, truly broken over our fight, took me to the hospital. I was pretty battered. The doctors knew what had happened to me and asked my husband to leave. They told me that I didn't have to go home and that I should report the incident to the police. Of course I didn't. As I mentioned earlier, we were both very angry people. I didn't want to go home right away from the hospital because my brother and his wife lived with us, and I couldn't let him see me in the state I was in. I stayed away as long as I could, waiting until I could heal. However, my brother had my kids and began to be concerned. The thought of my brother seeing me bandaged up frightened me because I knew he would go off and attack my husband. I also knew my husband had a gun and would no doubt use it to defend himself if my brother attacked him. Well, my fears became a reality.

My brother insisted that I come home or he would report me to child welfare. I had to go home. When I got out of the cab and my brother saw me, he lost it! My brother beat my husband mercilessly. When my husband had the opportunity, he went for his gun to protect himself and shot my brother five times. This horrid scenario played out right in front of our children. I collapsed at the bottom of our back stairs; I couldn't believe what had happened. My brother was lying on my hallway floor, bleeding and gasping for air. The messages began playing in my head: "See what you've done! Your wickedness has killed your baby brother."

Guilt ravaged my mind. My brother was a very popular singer, and one of the bullets had severed his vocal chords, which meant he could never sing again. I was shattered by it all, and I lost it! It was just too much for me, and my mind snapped! A nervous breakdown was inevitable and I was carted off to the psychiatric ward. It was just too much.

Later, there was the trial. I truly didn't want to be there. I knew that in spite of all that had happened to my brother, my husband had no choice but to defend himself. He could not be held liable for that very reason alone. But what was my family going to think? I had to get on the stand and offer the evidence. My brother and everyone would hate me because all my brother wanted to do was to get back at the person who had hurt me. How could I possibly live with myself? My brother would never sing again, and the only joy he had in his life was his singing career. I hated myself. I hated my life. I hated my aunt, who pushed me into this marriage when I was so young. I sank deeper into darkness and wanted my life to be over. "What good was it anyway?" the enemy taunted. "Your brother is going to hate you. Your husband hates you. Your father hates you. What's the use?" From what I could surmise of my life, he was right. It wasn't worth living. And where was God? Nowhere! Or so I thought. The prayers that my mother prayed for me and my brother were yet prevailing. My brother made a miraculous recovery and, to the surprise of everyone, got his beautiful voice back. As wonderful as that was, my life was no good. People gave God glory for the miracle, but at that point I had nothing to look forward to from God. My heart had become so hardened and my mind so clouded with lies that I would rather take my chances without Him.

After I was released from the psych ward, I would again attempt to take my life. As a matter of fact, I attempted suicide three times to be exact. I still have the marks on my wrists of one of those attempts. It serves as a constant reminder of how life's uncertain journey does not have to end in hopeless tragedy. I would later learn that there is hope because of our heavenly Father and His Son, Jesus Christ.

As I remember it, the courts ordered my husband to stay away from me, and that was all I needed! I was going to be on my own! And off into the dark world I went. All I truly wanted was to be in charge of my own life! I didn't want others telling me what I could or could not do, where I could and could not go! I wanted to run my life my own way. I was ready for the kind of life that was run by none other than me. I lived bold and as uncut as the Old Grandad bourbon that I drank!

The enemy of my soul was doing a great job of hardening my heart. I didn't realize what was happening to me.

However, that's how it is when you don't have the Light of the Truth to guide you. As far as I was concerned life had dealt me a bad stack of cards. The impending circumstances would only serve to callous my heart. Indeed, it became hard as rock. However, things were about to change. I was going to be tough enough to handle anything or anyone that came my way. I even figured that when my ex offered to pay for an apartment for me and the kids to live in, I was going to set him up really good. I suspected he probably felt guilty for all I had to deal with. He really wasn't a vicious man but, like me, had no light. One thing that he didn't know was the fact that I had my own pistol, and things were going to be a bit different. No one else was ever going to hurt me again. As far as I was concerned, the courts gave me a way out of my obligation to him. Now, my sights were set on what the world had to offer me.

What mattered to me was that I was free and had no obligation to him. All I had to look forward to was pure unadulterated fun, and I was going to live it up as much as I could! I got in with the wrong crowd and made friends with some tough drug dealers. I even promoted their wares. I was a pretty smooth dancer. I knew how to use my body. I was still quite young, felt pretty and sexy, and thought I was in total control of my destiny. Yet another lie of the enemy. However, no one could tell me what to do now. I was at the top of the world, or so I thought. I had come to that stage in my young life where, as my elders would say, I was smelling myself. I knew the power of being a woman, and I knew how to use what I had to get what I wanted. In my darkness, I sort of hoped someone would try me just so I could show them how tough I had become. Inside, I really wanted my ex to try something. I'm thankful to God that nothing happened. It would have only meant more tragedy, but I couldn't see it that way. I was blinded by arrogance and hatred. I tell you the truth—I was engulfed in pure, dark evil! It was nothing for me to go out and deliberately go after and seduce any man and think nothing of it! I knew the power of seduction quite well and used it to bring glory to myself! I had developed quite a lurid reputation. I don't know if my ex knew it, but I didn't care. Men worshipped my body, and I loved it. Lord, what in the world was I thinking? There I was, leading unsuspecting men into lustful idolatry, using my feminine wares as their temple of worship. Today, I thank God for the blood of Jesus that cleanses us from all unrighteousness. I can't stand to think how many souls were led to hell because of my wickedness. I know when I stand before my Lord there will be nothing to say except the name of Jesus.

It is not easy writing these things about myself, even though it is in my past. Dredging up what a wicked woman I was hurts. Remembering the darkness, the hatred, and out-of-control lifestyle I lived as a young woman still tears at my heart. Please know that I am not sharing my story in order to glory in those dark days. No, I write it because today I glory in the Lord Jesus Christ Who had mercy on my sad soul. He knew my pain and my struggle against forces that were much too powerful for me. He knew the powerful bondage that I was in, and He came after me. I want others who think there is no hope because of their past to know that is not true. There is hope in Jesus Christ. He makes all things new!

After I came to know Christ, I discovered this passage, which brought me to tears. It says, "But God showed His great love for us by sending Christ to die for us while we were still sinners" (Romans 5:8 NLT). While I was groveling in sin, Jesus still died for me so that I could be made whole, forgiven, and His. When I look back over my life and see what God has brought me through in spite of all my wickedness, I am so very grateful that He is real. I can never stop giving Him thanks for having mercy on me. I don't deserve His mercy, I know it! Yet, just as He went looking for Adam and Eve after they sinned in the garden, He came looking for even me.

Beloved, God *is* real. No matter what mistakes you have made in your life, they are not greater than God's love for you. There is no sin that Jesus didn't die for. His blood was the required payment to ransom our lives from Satan's trickery. The trick that began in the garden need not continue. The Light has come to push back the darkness. That Light is Jesus Christ. He came to set every captive free who Satan is holding in bondage to his lies. This freedom brings joy unspeakable and peace that passes human understanding. I tell my story because life's uncertain journey can actually turn out for your good. It did for me and my family. The beauty of God is He is not a respecter of persons. He has no favorites. Listen to this: according to John 17:23, He loves us just as much as He loves Jesus. I pray you not only hear this but believe it. You don't have to remain in darkness. The Light has come!

My young life was headed down a path of destruction while the enemy of my soul watched with glee, deceiving my mind with lies, keeping me blind to the dark pit that was awaiting me just a few yards ahead. I had no clue that I was like a sheep being carried to slaughter, unaware that there was someone leading me there. I was oblivious to how my life would impact my children.

2

DARKNESS RULED MY LIFE

*Then God said, "Let there be light," and there was
light. And God saw that the light was good. Then
He separated the light from the darkness.*

—Genesis 1:3–4 (NLT)

At twenty-five I thought I had learned a lot about life. I knew
what I wanted, and God was not on my list. I wasn't living the
high life, but I was in control, no one to tell me what I could
or could not do. I mentioned how my ex-husband got a place for me
and my kids to live. I believe he was really trying to make amends. But
as far as I was concerned, it was over. I had learned a few tricks of my
own. I knew how to pretend. I had figured out how to handle him. As
long as I gave him access to me and the children, things were good.
However, I had an ace in the hole. The courts had stated that he was
not supposed to be around me. Although we were still married, he
had no legal hold over me. I began to take action to deal with our
marital status, unbeknownst to him.

Upon my release from the psych ward, my best girlfriend came
to pick me up. It was my birthday, and she had a surprise for me. She
took me to meet a guy she said sold the best weed in Washington,
DC. He seemed to take a liking to me, so in my disturbed mind, I

began to plan and plot how I could get us more of this marijuana for free. My answer was to use what I had to get what I wanted. It had worked so many times before. The plot began. As I mentioned earlier, I was quite full of myself and had determined that there was no man that I couldn't seduce. I had already put in the paperwork for a divorce from my first husband. That would free the way for me to work on husband number two. After a couple of years of dating, the drug dealer was mine. He was used to having a lot of women around, but I figured none of them were as determined as I was. He seemed to be pretty street smart. He always had money on him, and he was tough! A real gangster if I had ever seen one. We became partners in crime and began a dark life of drugs, parties...you name it. I literally jumped out of the frying pan and into the fire!

I was able to get my own apartment. It literally was on the thirteenth floor. The button on the elevator said it was the eleventh floor, but it was actually the thirteenth floor. Me and my drug-dealer friend moved in together. I didn't know it at the time, but he was legally blind. The dark glasses he wore were actually medically prescribed. He may have been blind, but he was also not a man to mess with. If my husband came around trying to threaten me, he was going to have a problem. My new friend really loved me and my children. He had such a way with them, and they grew to love him. In the street he was not the man to mess with, but with the kids, he was clay in their hands. One day, after one of our drunken nights, he asked me to marry him. By then my divorce was final so—why not! Would you believe that after three days of marriage we were back at the justice of the peace seeking an annulment? The judge told us we were stuck with each other.

We were a sad case too—both of us. The only thing I had worth anything were my three precious gems. They had endured so very much. However, I had no idea that even yet my mother's prayers were being answered and the Lord was about to put His divine foot right in the middle of my mess. Well, in the middle of our criminal enterprise, I was attempting to raise three children. Even though I didn't believe all those hell-fire Bible stories I had learned as a child, they

were useful to help keep my kids in line. I decided my children needed to hear that: You'd better be good or you are going to hell where
the devil is and there is endless fire. I believed that it would work.
I sent them to the resident Sunday school in the Section 8 housing
high-rise complex where we lived. It was a great convenience!

I was not the kind of person who was going out of my way to seek
an experience with God. I really didn't know Him, remember. As a
matter of fact, on the morning that I encountered the God of my
mother, I was drunk and enjoying some good marijuana. I was not
listening to a great message that touched my heart. Nor had I visited
one of those Holy Ghost–fire church services that had impacted me
so profoundly that I wanted to change my life.

However, on one of those Sunday mornings, my youngest son
spoke under the inspiration of the Holy Spirit. God had given him
the boldness to ask me a question. He asked me why I sent them
to Sunday school but didn't go myself. Wrong day, sonny! Previously
we had gone out to the twenty-four-seven liquor store to purchase a
half gallon of Johnny Walker Red. I already had fixed their breakfast
and began our Sunday-morning binge, and so I was not in the mood
for insolence. I cursed at my son and frightened him a bit. He was
used to my cursing tirades; however, I don't think he expected my
response to such an honest question. My response was so abrupt that
he dropped his little Bible. I sent him on his way without allowing
him to get his Bible.

There on my bedroom floor laid his small, white Bible. I really
didn't want to move, but I was bothered by seeing that Bible lying on
the floor. I went over to pick it up. It had fallen facedown and open
to a page that I felt compelled to read. It was Isaiah chapter 12 (KJV).
As my eyes caught a glimpse of the words, I could hear the voice of
the Lord speaking aloud to me. "And in that day thou shalt say, O
Lord, I will praise thee: though thou was angry with me, thine anger
is turned away, and thou comfortedst me." As I read, I heard the Lord
saying, "Nadine, I am not angry with you. I love you. Then tears began to form in my eyes, and I fell to my knees in a crying fit. All of a

sudden, I was sober! I just heard God speak to me, and it wasn't the weed or the alcohol.

What was happening to me? How could these words be so powerfully penetrating that they could cause me to tremble, fall to my knees, and weep? My mind began to race, frantically attempting to understand what was going on inside me.

At that moment, I recalled the scene years before during my first marriage when my ex-husband purchased the portrait of Satan and hung it in our living room. On one of those drug trips we would take, I had a lively conversation with the devil. He promised me a lot and warned me that I must never pray. He told me that God hated me and would strike me down dead on the spot if I prayed to Him. As a result, I never prayed, fearful that God would strike me dead. It became my method of operation...crazy. As I mentioned earlier, I had several stints on the psych ward to prove it.

However, on that fateful morning, I heard the Lord speaking to me through Isaiah, saying, "Nadine, I am not angry with you. I love you. Although I was angry with you, my anger has turned away, and I will comfort you." As I read, the words just came to life for me. I couldn't stop reading! As I read it, I felt as if a cascade of refreshing water was flowing over me, cleansing me and nourishing my soul. The Lord knew exactly what I needed to hear. No one else knew of that hallucinogenic encounter with the devil, but God did, and He spoke directly to it. He knew the lie the enemy had planted in my mind and wanted me to know the truth that He was *not* angry with me! That morning I prayed to my Father and He heard me. My heart was filled with unspeakable joy, and I began to praise and worship His glory. I couldn't stop crying and praising Him. For the first time, I experienced the Love of God in a very profound way. When I arose from my tears, I was a different person.

Now, my poor, unsuspecting new hubby slept throughout that encounter. He had no idea that the woman who was waiting for him when he awoke was not the same woman who was with him when he fell asleep. He was simply floored by it all.

What's up with this? We were partners in crime, and he couldn't understand what had happened. I couldn't even explain it. It was as if God decided that on this day He would put His foot smack dab in the middle of our lives. It was on that October morning God decided to put a stop to the dangerously decadent lifestyle we had chosen to live. The Lord turned me completely around. My husband didn't like it at all. I stopped drinking, smoking, partying; I was no longer interested in those things. All hell broke loose in my home and my marriage. My hubby and I were now mortal enemies. He was not going to be a part of that "holy rolling," as he called it.

The next fifteen years were the most painful, trying, and yet exhilarating years of my life. I suffered much because of the lies of the enemy; however, I witnessed the power of God and saw His mighty hand move time and time again on my behalf. I often tell women I disciple that if I had to do it all over again, I would. Through those years of having to fellowship with Christ's suffering, I ultimately experienced the resurrection power of God at work in my life.

3

LET THERE BE LIGHT

And God said, Let there be light.

—Genesis 1:3 (KJV)

This testimony is written to convey to everyone that no matter how evil or how wicked or how vile or how low you have fallen, your heavenly Father loves you with an everlasting love. Please know that whatever you may have done or may be experiencing right now, your Father is standing by, ready to help you.

After giving my life to Christ, my son's little white Bible became mine. I was so hungry to know, hear, and learn more about my mother's God. I remember telling Him that I didn't know very much about Him, but I wanted to learn more. I asked Him to help me get to know Him better. He did not disappoint me! I devoured that Bible and began to depend upon it for answers. What I learned was that the story of Israel's relationship and journey with God was the same as my spiritual relationship and journey with Him. I discovered that just as God brought Israel out of Egyptian bondage, He was doing the same for me. He totally convinced me that He delivered us both because He loved us and desired to dwell among us. I may not have been born a literal Jew, but I learned that spiritually I am no different than a Jew. The same Love God had for Abraham, Isaac, and Jacob, He has for me.

Theologians have determined that grace is the unmerited favor of God. I have found it to be so much more! It is born out of His everlasting love for us. God has a fierce and tenacious love for His children. Scriptures reveal His attitude and the nature of His love for us. I cannot describe the level of joy I experienced when I discovered that He had rigged life's uncertain journey to work out in our favor (Rom. 8:28).

Realistically, life is a battle. No one can be breathing and not have figured that out. But for every born-again child of God, the battle has not only been rigged in our favor, but it has actually already been won! You see, Jesus took care of everything. "When He had disarmed the rulers and authorities [those supernatural forces of evil operating against us], He made a public example of them [exhibiting them as captives in His triumphal procession], having triumphed over them through the cross" (Colossians 2:15 AMP). Yes, I thank God the Father for the victory He has provided us through Jesus Christ our Lord!

I began to experience this wonderful Grace when I realized that while I was defaming God and refusing to believe in His Son, His grace was yet being extended to me. While I was cursing and carousing through life, the price had already been paid for my forgiveness. I walked around in total ignorance and darkness, being held in that bondage for thirty-two years of my life. That is, until the Father said, "Let there be light." At that moment Jesus showed up and set this captive free!

I remember Him telling me one time during one of our infamous conversations that sin is not greater than He is. There was no deed or act that I had committed that was greater than Him or His love for me. He asked me if any of my children had been born handicapped or deficient in some area if I would cast them out into the street to fend for themselves? Of course not, my love for them would cause me to protect them all the more. As the scripture says, "If we being evil know how to give good things to our children, how much more will our heavenly Father give good things to those who ask?" (Matt. 7:11 KJV). He provided us with His "Good Thing;" His name is Jesus!

I have been walking with the Lord for many years, and I am still quite amazed at His love, grace, and mercy toward me. It just takes my breath away every time I think, Who am I that He would be mindful of me? My life before He showed up was rife in wickedness, hatred, anger, bitterness, and rage. How could such a bitter and evil woman merit the love and favor of such a loving God? Yet I tell you the truth, God loves us because He can't help it! You see, God *is love!* That's Who He is! That is the character of our heavenly Father. Not only is He love, but He loves His children. And like any good parent, He is grieved by our disbelief of His love for us, always wanting the best for us yet having to watch us muddle through life without even knowing He is there. But beloved, He *is* there! He is right there with you, standing over you, providing protection, covering, and guidance, and we are just oblivious to His presence, His love, and His grace. I learned that God wasn't angry with me, like the devil had told me, and He had no desire to destroy or kill me, not at all. What He wanted me to experience was the "newness of life," a life that, though not issue-free, was filled with righteousness, peace, and joy! Unspeakable joy! Peace that would surpass all my understanding! He taught me that I had been given both power and authority over all the power of my enemy (Luke 10:19). He gave me the confidence to know that when I called upon Him, He would answer me, not so much because I was righteous. I learned that truly I have no righteousness of my own. The righteousness I was given belongs to His Son! Our righteousness, the Word declares, is like filthy tampons! (Isa. 64:6) Gross, yet true! No, it's all because He is a merciful, loving Father. Scripture goes on to say that it is "not by works of righteousness which we have done (or do), but according to *His **mercy*** He saved us, by the washing of regeneration, and renewing of the Holy Ghost" (Titus 3:5 KJV).

I knew I deserved the anger and punishment of God. I did everything I was big and bad enough to do, and yet His Word spoke and declared to me: "But now, (Nadine), listen to the Lord who created you… the one who formed you says, "Do not be afraid, for I have ransomed you, I have called you by name; *you are mine*! (Isa. 43:1,(NLT) emphasis and additions mine). He went on to say to me (as I paraphrase what I heard), "I chose you in Christ before the foundation of the world, that you should be holy and without blame before me in love!" (Ephesians 1:4 KJV). Did you hear that! My mouth dropped once again as I read and heard these powerful words. I was holy and without blame. My mind went to racing. I knew that holy things belong to God. There is no other venue for having or possessing holy things without God making it so. He called me holy and then, as I envisioned the enemy of my soul going up before the Father to accuse me of all my wrongdoings, Jesus stands up and tells him to hush! You can lay no blame to her charge because I took care of it all for her, once and for all! Never again will you bring accusation against her to my Father; she is not to blame! This grace is so powerful that He won't allow the enemy to put blame on me. Now, if that's not rigging the fight, I don't know what is. But guess what...He is God! He is the Supreme Ruler of all things! He does as He pleases. And believe me when He says we are not to be blamed, who can challenge His Word? Paul says, "Who dares accuse us whom God has chosen for His own? There is no one—for God Himself has given us right standing with Himself (Romans 8:33 NLT). Once again I fell into a sobbing heap! God's Word began to penetrate my heart with such force and power that all I could do was weep. I was weakened and humbled by this revelation of God's unmerited favor and love toward me. Who, I ask, is like the Lord? I don't know how old you are as you read this book, but an old Christian song began to well up in my heart: "Can't nobody do me like Jesus!" Nobody!

I am speaking about experiencing God's grace and the strength, confidence, and hope it provided to me while I was yet in the midst of my struggles. The enemy's degrading tirade of demeaning words to me and about me were not silenced but had no power over me anymore! God had allowed His glorious Light to shine truth on the enemy and his lies. He would have a hard time convincing me of his lies! I now am armed with the Truth, better known as Sword of the Spirit, which is the Word of God! From now on I would accept what is written as what is true about me, about life, about the circumstances that surrounded me. I began to realize that they had the expressed purpose of drawing me away from my God and into a web of lies designed to defeat me and ultimately cause me to call my Father a liar! He began to teach me how to fight the good fight of faith. This faith was given to me by my Father. I learned to have more faith in His Word.

Beloved, know this: Were it not for the grace of God, we would have already been consumed, wiped out, and destroyed! God's grace provides us with time to recognize this and repent. It provides us with room to stumble and make mistakes with the knowledge that we can get back up! "It is the Lord's mercies that we are not consumed, because His compassions fail not. They are new every morning; great is Thy faithfulness" (Lam. 3:22–23 KJV). Yes, every morning when you awake, new mercy awaits you. Yes, God gives us all a space of time to repent. However, because we don't know the Lord's timing, it behooves us to repent the moment we are made aware of our transgression. Don't become complacent and even think, Well, the Lord must be held up with other things, so I've got time. No beloved, "the Lord is not slack concerning His promise, as some men count slackness; but is long-suffering to us-ward, not willing that any should perish, but that all should come to repentance. But the day of the Lord will come as a thief in the night; in the which the heavens shall pass away with a great noise, and the elements shall melt with fervent heat, the earth also and the works that are therein shall be burned up" (2 Pet. 3:9–10). You really think global warming won't have its consequences on this planet? You just read it described in God's word. It going to go down just as God warned us it would. You don't want to take the chance of not believing Him. Now is the time to receive Him as your King.

Beloved, one of the greatest things I developed out of experiencing the power of God's grace was a grateful heart. The grace of God produced gratitude and thankfulness in me. You know why? I could have died in my sin! I could have lost everything. I grew to understand that had not my Father loved me, covered me, and kept me by answering my mother's prayers, I would not have lived to see my children become adults, marry, and give me precious grandchildren. All of that would have been taken away from me, and oh so much more. Oh how grateful I am that God is not only real but He loves me! You'll hear me say that over and over again! God *is* real, and I am so thankful that He loved me enough to let me know it. He didn't leave me to my own foolish devices but literally came after me—not just once but a second time.

4

BUT, GOD

*But God, who is rich in mercy, for His
great love wherewith He loved us.*

—Ephesians 2:4 (KJV)

Y ou see, I have experienced the love of God throughout my
life's journey. My story may lead some to believe I became
this wonderful godly woman. The Lord saved me all right,
but there was yet much for me to learn. You see, I stumbled and fell
greatly during my time of testing. That's right! We will all be tested,
just as Israel was tested by God in the wilderness (Deut. 8:2).

When I was a babe in Christ, God treated me with great care, as you
would a young child. I had witnessed some very powerful miracles as a
young woman in the faith. However, it was time for me to grow up! It was
time to discover what my faith was made of and if I truly trusted God.

I grew to truly love the Lord very deeply and wanted nothing more
than to please Him. After finding the right church, I began to get the
sense of a deeper calling on my life. I attended a Christian training college for four years after I gave my life to the Lord. It was there that He
taught me faith. The bishop and his wife were my spiritual mom and
pop. God used his wife to teach me God's Word! This dynamic duo, as
we called them, had a powerful faith ministry, and God had directed

me to their church to learn some things. Bishop was a strong man of God, full of the Word, and boy, could he preach. His wife had the divine gift of a teacher. I enrolled myself and my children into their Christian school, and we were on our journey of faith in Christ together.

After Christian school I went on to ministerial school and was ultimately ordained in ministry. God then gave me a vision for the Caravan of Love ministry. I had a dream that revealed a day, somewhere around Christmas, in which I saw a huge caravan of cars, vans, and buses, all loaded up with toys, food, and clothes. This caravan traveled through the troubled neighborhoods of Washington, DC, dropping off food, toys, and clothing to these desperately poor neighborhoods. I saw mommas crying as they watched their kids pull toys and things from the caravan. They were filled with such joy because they knew they could not have afforded to give their children a decent Christmas. It was a very powerful dream. However, I would later learn that it was a little more than a just a dream. It ultimately became my ministry unto the Lord. Now, when God gave me the dream, I was living in Section 8 housing, hardly able to feed my own children, much less anyone else's. However, the fragrance of this dream would not leave me. It just kept nagging away at me. Nagging, because I could see no way for me to accomplish this dream.

Then one day one of the community leaders and managers of the building where I lived approached me and asked if I would help get our Mayor reelected. I had become quite involved in my community and had assisted him in creating a tenants' association in the building he managed. Ultimately I was voted in as the association's president. Well, I wasn't a fan of our Mayor so I declined his offer. However, the Lord brought the dream before me once again. I believed that He wanted me to say yes to this offer. I couldn't imagine why, but I obeyed. God told me to share my dream with this man and tell him that if the mayor would support such an endeavor, he could regain the confidence of the community, which could possibly lead to his reelection. Well, to my surprise he liked the idea! I was contacted by one of the mayor's assistants, who asked me to come down to his office to share my vision/dream to get the

Mayor reelected. That's not exactly what I had agreed to do but that's how I suppose it was communicated to them. Anyway, after sharing my idea the Mayor's assistant thought it was a wonderful idea. Then he asked the million-dollar question, "How much money has been raised already". Money! What money!

"Well, he asked, haven't you started collecting funds and donations for the event?"

"No sir," I replied.

"Well, how do you plan to pull all this off?" My response floored him. I told him that I had no idea! All I knew was I believed that God had given me a dream and a vision, and if it was something that He wanted to happen, He would make it so. "You mean you are depending on God to pull this off?"

"Yes, sir," I replied.

Well, that was it. He had been misinformed and was under the impression that I had all these people backing me with this project. So, the mayor's assistant thanked me for my time and sent me on my way. However, before I could get to the elevators, someone came running after me.

"Miss Davis…Miss Davis, can you come back to the office, please?"

When I got back to the assistant's office, he sat at his desk with his head in his hands and said, "I don't know why I'm doing this, but I've got to help you with this."

I was floored! Not only was this dream going to become a reality, but the Lord had commissioned the government to help me. Well, sure enough, on December 23, 1985, the Caravan of Love took to the streets of Washington, DC. The response was overwhelming! The DC Van club donated vans and churches sent their members and buses—it was spectacular to say the least. But if that wasn't miracle enough, on the day we were to launch, there was a warning of an impending snow storm. However, as long as the caravan was rolling, the sun shined bright. But the moment we returned to our launch site, prayed, and said our good-byes, the snow came down like crazy!

Well, that was my maiden ministry launch. We went on to conduct the caravans for about five more years, with the help and assistance of the DC government. Now, if that was not a time of God's demonstration of His great power, the follow-up sealed the deal for me. It became a regular thing, these dreams and visions. And on one particular Sunday, I had been invited to hear a young Nigerian pastor preach at one of the churches that was so instrumental in helping with the caravan. The church was packed, and everyone was so excited to hear this young man speak. After a powerful time of praise, I sat down with the woman who had invited me. However, I never got to hear the sermon this young man preached.

While yet wide awake, I had a dream. In this dream I was walking through a beautiful grass-covered place. The sun shone brightly, birds were chirping, and I could hear something that sounded like preaching off in the distance. As I walked toward the sound, I looked up on a hill and saw someone preaching the Word under a tin-covered structure. As I glanced over my shoulder, there was a brick pit with smoke coming out of it. There were a couple of women cooking fish in a huge pot. Off to my right were children playing and running around. I also saw what looked like a small pond, and people were getting baptized in it. It was such a glorious place, and I had no idea where I was. So I looked up to heaven, as it seemed to open up above me. It was funny that I wasn't afraid, but I asked, "Lord, what is this place?"

I heard, "This is My day. This is your day, a day of great revival."

The next thing I knew, everyone was standing up, applauding the speaker, who I never heard. I was a bit startled because it seemed no one paid me any attention. Had I fallen asleep or something? Well, I went over to meet the young man. I had to apologize for not really hearing much of his sermon, but congratulated him. I had not known at that time that God would unite us in ministry together.

Well, upon leaving the church, I couldn't wait to tell the woman who had invited me about this strange dream I had while I was still awake. She was very moved by the dream and asked me what I thought it was all about. I had no clue. Well, as time went on, I began to share that dream with others. I didn't know what else to do, but I did remember how God used the first dream and brought it to pass. I had every reason to believe

He was going to do it again. I shared the dream with my pastor and asked her for prayer. Then, *bam!* I clearly knew that the day that God revealed was going to take place on my birthday. I was to surrender that day over to Him because He was going to show up. But I was still uncertain how to find this place. My friend had suggested Rock Creek Park, which was a popular outdoor site in Washington, DC. But the place I saw in my vision didn't look like a park. Lo and behold, the day came when God decided to reveal to me where the location was.

My friend who had invited me to the church service the day I received the vision told me that her niece knew where the location might be. I questioned it because I did not recall seeing her niece anywhere in the vision. However, I suggested we go see it. My friend and I were directed to Brandywine, Maryland. I was not very familiar with the area. We had been given an address and some directions. The location I stopped at seemed to be a regular street. I saw no place for a park. However, we discovered a path that seemed to lead up into a clearing. I asked my friend to take a walk up the drive path and let me know what she thought. Well, when she walked back to the car, she had tears in her eyes. She could hardly speak.

"What's wrong?" I asked.

She replied, "You have got to come see this. You are not going to believe it." She got into the car, and we drove onto this path. As I entered into this huge open plot of land, I could not believe my eyes. It was the exact place I had visited in my dreams, complete with a pond, a brick pit, and a tin tent on a hill. "Lord Jesus," I cried, "who is sufficient for such things?"

We wandered up to what looked like a ranch house off to the side. As we went up to the door, an elderly man came out. We introduced ourselves, and I shared the dream with him and his elderly wife. She, however, was not surprised. She said she knew I was coming. They told me if I wanted to use their property, they would be honored to have us. When I asked her how much she would charge, she said there was no charge. As I described the event to them, her husband said he would build some steps down into the pond so we could easily enter it for baptisms. He rigged electricity to the tin hut so we could hear the messages being preached. I tell you, I was floored by it all.

But there were yet more miracles to be seen! Not only did the revival take place on my birthday but on the very morning of the revival, it rained cats and dogs. Actually, if I remember correctly, the rain started the night before. Well, first thing that morning, my pastor called and asked me if I had set a rain date for the revival. I told her that the Lord never gave me one. I told her that this was the day God gave me in my dream. I trusted Him to do something about the rain and the mud it had produced. Well, I had invited three ministers to meet me at the property early that morning so that we could pray and consecrate the grounds. As we drove down the drive path, our car tires were covered in mud. They looked at me and wondered aloud if this was a good idea. I recalled my drive down to Brandywine that morning. As I prayed and called upon the Lord for answers I began to see blue skies. It was raining like crazy, but somehow I saw blue skies. That was sufficient for me. The Lord showed me blue skies, so that was what I expected to see. So, we gathered in a circle and began to pray. As we were praying, I prayed based on what the Lord had revealed, blue skies.

I heard the Spirit of the Lord encouraging me by saying, "Elijah prayed, and it rained. He also prayed for it to stop. So, as I began to pray, I commanded the clouds to part to the east and to the west, that the rain would cease, and that the glorious light of the sun would shine forth. When we finished praying, it rained for about fifteen more minutes! Then, a ray of sunshine peeked out from the clouds. By the time the first car showed up, the sun was completely out. Before we knew it, the ground was dry and hard. When Bishop and his wife arrived, she walked up to me and said, "Look at little Elijah." How did she know what the Lord had told me? It was the confirmation I needed to carry me through that day.

As if that wasn't enough! We had hundreds of people show up. So many that I knew I didn't have enough food to feed all of them. I had purchased seven packs of fish, seven loaves of bread, seven packs of hot dogs, seven packs of buns, seven heads of lettuce, seven tomatoes, and seven cases of soda. That was all I could afford. Anyway, I only invited my church home family and my ministerial class. Altogether, I had not anticipated more than about one hundred people. However, there must have been close to three hundred people who showed up that day. My husband would say five hundred, but many more than we had anticipated. Yes, my husband, though not sober, accompanied me that day. He was there to see the mighty work of the God that I served and loved so much. He witnessed how the little food we brought proved to be more than enough for those attending. As a matter of fact, once the day was over and people began to leave, there was so much food left, we had to give it away!

Some guests came to the revival drunk. I didn't know who had invited them. However, when those who asked to be baptized began to approach the pond, something miraculous happened. A ministerial school teacher, who was also my teacher, poured anointing oil into the pond to bless it. As soon as the oil hit the water, a colorful rainbow appeared in the water as ripples cascaded throughout the pond. As people saw this, they began to ooh and aww at the sight of it. Before we knew it, those drunken men came forth and asked to be baptized, giving their lives to Jesus at the sight of what had just happened with the water. I can't begin to recall how many were saved that day. Indeed, it was a day of great revival and miracles galore!

My purpose in sharing these great and wonderful miracles from God serves as the precursor to explain why the Lord had to rescue me again. You see, after this great and powerful display of God's love and power, the Caravan of Love began to grow, and God began to reveal Himself to me even more.

I continued to serve the community with our Christmas Caravan of Love. We had been living in Section 8 housing, but God was about to do something wonderful for me and my family.

During one of my many Bible studies, I came across a passage of scripture that said, "When the Son of Man returns, will He find faith in the earth?" (Luke 18:8 KJV). All I knew was the fact that if Jesus asked this question, it must be something very important. What it revealed to me was the fact that if Jesus asked that question, faith was something I really needed. So, I began to pray and seek the Lord for the gift of faith. I believe that is why He sent me to the church I attended. They understood and taught about faith.

After the great revival experience, my pastor's wife discerned that this was one of the spiritual gifts that God had imparted to me. However, I would later learn that faith that has not been tested isn't genuine faith. God would use my Pastor's wife to teach me more about faith. Then, He would provide the trials that would almost shatter that faith.

During one of our classes, my pastor had each of us write down five things we wanted to receive by faith from the Lord. The first thing on my list was my husband's salvation. The last thing on the list was a house. All but one of those items on my list was granted before the year was out. I had really thought the hardest thing on my list was the house. It turned out to be my husband's salvation.

This was my second marriage. I had really messed up the first one and wanted this one to bring Him glory. I recalled a time when my ex-husband taunted me with the notion that God did not honor divorce and that I was living in sin with this new husband. It caused me great concern because the Lord had been so good to me. I didn't want to come all this way by faith only to find out my marriage was unholy. So, I cried out to the Lord for answers. I had seen Him doing such great things in my life, how could He have permitted me to marry this man? Well, as was His fashion, He led me to a passage in scripture. I read that "each of you should continue to live in whatever situation the Lord has placed you, and remain as you were when God first called you. This is my rule for all the churches. For instance, a man who was circumcised before he became a believer should not try to reverse it. And the man who was uncircumcised when he became a believer should not be circumcised now. For it makes no difference whether or not a man has been circumcised. The important thing is to keep God's commandments. Yes, each of you should remain as you were when God called you" (1 Corinthians 7:17–20 KJV). There was my answer. It was when I remarried that God saved and called me. I was not to seek to get out of this marriage but believe that God would save him too.

It was not long after writing that list that one of the mothers at my church had her daughter call me to tell me that she had seen a beautiful house for me and my family. It was such a cute little corner townhouse, complete with a backyard for my kids. Yes! There was only one problem. There was a Sold sign in the yard. Well, after seeing the Lord shut up the rain and feed over three hundred people with leftovers—so what! My girlfriend and I took some anointing oil, anointed the house, and walked around it seven times in the name of the Lord and declared the house mine. As we were ending up our prayer, a gentleman came out of the house. He asked if I was interested in it. Of course, I said yes. He then went on to say that sometimes people put contracts on homes that don't always go through and asked if I wanted to submit an application in the event the contract didn't work. I did, and eleven months thereafter, my family moved into that home.

Once God blessed us with our own home, I opened up my new home and launched the Caravan of Love Community Outreach right there in southeast Washington, DC. About sixty-five children from the community enrolled in our weekly Bible study in my home. I felt that since the Lord had provided us the miracle of home ownership, this house would be used for His glory. After all, He was the One who provided it, down payment and all!

It was a time of great joy to see God work so mightily on our behalf. Even after giving us a brand-new home, the miracles did not stop coming. I recall one miracle in particular. I wanted to be able to transport the children who attended our community Bible Study on trips and needed a van. I prayed and asked the Lord about it. Lo and behold, a wonderful man of God, who also served as Office Friendly from the police department, called and asked me if I knew anyone who needed a van. I told him I did. He told me if I could come up with $7,000, I could have it. Well, that was a lot of money for this poor woman who could just keep her mortgage paid and support this little community ministry. However, I told him to hold the van for me because I believed that God would provide.

A few days later, a gentleman I had met at one of our prayer meetings knocked on my door. As I welcomed him into my home, he looked sternly at me and said, "Ms. Nadine, there is something you need from the Lord. You are to tell me what it is—no matter how big it is." Wow, it didn't take me any time to know that God had sent this man. So, I told him I needed $7,000 for a new van. He thanked me, turned, and left my home. Wow! That was powerful! Once again I fell into a weeping heap, amazed again by the love of my Father. Not really knowing how this would play out, patience had to have its perfect work in me.

I can't remember just how long it was, but a few days afterward, there was another knock on my door. It was this same man. He extended an envelope to me, with a huge smile on his face. I began to weep before I opened it. There it was! A certified check for $7,000!

These, and the many miracles I experienced under the loving care of my Father, were the undergirding I would need to help build my faith and endurance for the great lessons I was about to learn about this wonderful salvation that comes by grace through faith (Eph. 2:8). I was going to need this grace, coupled with great faith, because I was about to be tested. God was going to use my second husband to test my faith.

Despite all that God was doing through my life and ministry, I had not yet experienced victory in my marriage. My husband was the first item written on my faith list to God at Jericho Christian College. I had received four of my five requests. He had also confirmed that the fifth request would be fulfilled through a dream. In this dream, I was looking out a window and could hear my husband's voice. However, I could not see him. He was in a dark alleyway, but I could hear him as his voice became louder. As I watched, I saw my husband stepping out of the dark alleyway into the sunlight. However, as I looked on, I saw that there were people following him out of the dark alley. I then heard the Lord say, "This is how I am going to use your husband's life." Well, after having experienced how God worked through my dreams before, my expectation was my husband would be joining me in faith very soon. I had hoped it would have happened before we got the house, but God had His own plan. In fact, from the time He revealed the dream and promised to save my husband until the time it actually happened was almost fifteen years!

Truly, being so young in faith, I was oblivious to the plan that would ultimately play out in my life. I was totally unaware of the battles that awaited me that would test my young faith.

Happy and excited about receiving the home I had put on my list, I truly wanted to show my gratitude to the Lord by serving Him all the more.

So off I went, attempting to serve the Lord and share Christ with as many in my community as I could. However, my husband was just getting worse and worse. He was becoming more of the son of Belial than I had ever imagined. He was doing every kind of wicked thing you could imagine. How could I possibly maintain any level of respect and support from my community with his shenanigans? It was difficult enough being a woman in ministry at a time when that was not very popular. I had battles to fight without, not desiring to also have battles to fight from within. What was the matter with him? He had witnessed God's power taking place. He saw the same miracles I did. Why was he not submitting to Christ? He didn't even try to hide all his evil deeds. Everyone who knew us knew what I had to deal with. Too often I would hear, "We are praying for you, Sister Davis." Too often I would cry out to the Lord, "How long, Lord? How long?"

You know, the apostle Paul accomplished great and mighty things after his conversion. However, like Paul, we must learn the full spectrum of truth of this salvation that The Lord has provided for us. Paul put it this way: "That I may know Him [*experientially, becoming more thoroughly acquainted with Him, understanding the remarkable wonders of His Person more completely*] and [*in that same way experience*] the power of His resurrection [*which overflows and is active in believers*], and [*that I may share*] the fellowship of His sufferings, by being *continually* conformed [*inwardly into His likeness even*] to His death [*dying as He did*]." (Philippians 3:10 AMP)

Yes, I had experienced many powerful manifestations of God's Power as He revealed great wonders to me. The apostle Paul explains it this way: "That experience is worth boasting about, but I'm not going to do it. I will boast only about my weaknesses. If I wanted to boast, I would be no fool in doing so, because I would be telling the truth. But I won't do it, because I don't want anyone to give me credit beyond what they can see in my life or hear in my message, even though I have received such wonderful revelations from God. So to keep me from becoming proud, I was given a thorn in my flesh, a messenger from Satan to torment me and keep me from becoming proud. Three different times I begged the Lord to take it away. Each time he said, 'My grace is all you need. My power works best in weakness.' So now I am glad to boast about my weaknesses, so that the power of Christ can work through me. That's why I take pleasure in my weaknesses and in the insults, hardships, persecutions, and troubles that I suffer for Christ. For when I am weak, then I am strong" (2 Cor. 12:5–10 NLT). By the multitude of miracles I had witnessed, my faith was strengthened greatly. However, that would not be the hallmark of my relationship with the Lord. Like Paul, I had to learn to die, to humble myself. I had to learn to yield myself in obedience to this death I had been called to die. I would ultimately learn these things through suffering.

It isn't clear in the scripture if Paul's thorn in the flesh was actually a physical ailment or a harassing individual, but in either case, Paul asked that this "thorn in the flesh" be removed and taken away. In my case, I learned what my thorn in the flesh would be. It would be my husband. But before I go on, let me just say that today I bear witness to the reality of this truth written in scripture! God's grace is sufficient! For when I thought I just couldn't take any more, God's loving grace became my sufficiency. That grace was extended to me through Jesus Christ, my Lord. Yes, I learned how to suffer for Christ, but it was because of the blessings that came from it that I no longer seek to sidestep the suffering. I would go through it over and over again because of the great gain it afforded me and because the Lord is the One Who gets the Glory.

As I had shared earlier, after my new life began, my husband and I became mortal enemies. I had not begun to hate him; I just didn't like him anymore. He wanted to continue to live a life of sin, and I didn't! He wanted to continue drinking, carousing, and partying—I didn't. However, I didn't want him to do those things either. I wanted him serving God with me.

However, as time went on, it was becoming quite obvious that he wasn't going to change. I had even been admonished by those who were shepherding me that I should consider divorce. They said that I was unequally yoked together with an unbeliever who also was an adulterer. I agreed. Scripture provided a way for me to be free of this toxic relationship (1 Cor. 7:10–11, 2 Cor. 6:14). But as I mentioned, I had the habit of getting confirmation for things spoken to advise me. I asked the Lord if He would sanction such a divorce. He said no! He shared that He had waited patiently for me to come to my senses. It was now my turn to do the same for my husband. He then gave me a scripture that I was to pray over him. I was to pray according to Ephesians 1:17-19 which said that that the Lord would give my husband the spirit of wisdom and revelation in the knowledge of Him, that the eyes of his understanding may be enlightened, that he would know what the hope of his calling is, and what the riches of his inheritance was, the exceeding greatness of His power to us who believe. He assured me that He would provide me with the ability to bear all things, believe all things, hope all things, and endure all things (1 Cor. 13:7).

Well, all right then. I had a decision to make. I would either believe the advice of men or God. I chose to believe God. Before you begin to applaud, please know that this decision came at a great price, one that would almost cost me my life. For those of you who know and have met my husband, you have never met the man I will share with you. You haven't because the man that I am now married to is a totally different person. God took the Nabal (1 Sam. 25:3) I had married and transformed him into a prince!

Not long after my salvation, I recall an incident when I was pregnant with my youngest son. I had gone looking for my husband in the high-rise Section 8 housing complex where we lived. I knew it wouldn't be hard to find him because, coming from the hills of Pennsylvania, he had a very loud voice. So, I walked down the corridors of one floor after another until I heard him: "You go on, girl!" Well, I knocked on the door, and a young woman with a white negligee answered. I asked if John was there, and she let me in. There he was, sitting at her dining-room table, lighting a joint of marijuana. Well, suffice it to say that I lost it! I yanked him up by his shirt collar and escorted him from her apartment. As I marched him back up to our apartment, I had some pretty tart words for him.

Some of his friends heard about what had happened and came to his rescue. They were at my apartment door, insisting that I calm down because of my pregnancy. I was steaming, and I didn't want to calm down. I wanted him to feel the full brunt of my pain, and I didn't care who heard it! I didn't want any of their advice because they obviously knew about it and kept it from me. Lo and behold, I did wind up being hospitalized briefly. However, the food for thought the enemy was providing me was excruciatingly more painful to bear. How could he do this to me? My mind raced as I was reminded of the prayer I had prayed just so this man could have a son. This was our miracle baby. He didn't know it, but I had already had two abortions, and my body had been rendered incapable of becoming pregnant. Before Christ entered my life, that physical malady worked out quite well for me. No more need for birth control! It wasn't a life-threatening situation, but it was also not life bearing either. However, after marrying my husband and experiencing the Love of God, I so wanted to give him a son. He had already fathered several children in his youth, but he didn't know where they were, nor was he involved in their lives. So, as far as I was concerned, he didn't have any offspring. So, I prayed and asked the Lord for a son for my new husband. Well, he answered me, and I became pregnant.

After all that, here he was smoking pot with this scantily clad woman of ill repute. He knew I was having a very difficult pregnancy. Because of my physical condition, the doctor had to watch me closely. I was bedridden for much of my pregnancy. So, how could he do this to me? But really, what was I to expect? Did I really think carrying his child would change him in any way? Only Jesus can change a man's heart. I learned that I still held some vestiges of the world's view and culture dancing around in my head. That old ghetto lie that "if you have his baby, he will love you" never has worked and never will. Anyway, suffice it to say, the Lord heard my prayer, and on July 22, 1979, our little brown bomber was born.

Years and years had gone by since the Lord had saved my soul. Miracles and blessings were bestowed upon me in spite of all my husband was doing. I had tried everything possible to maintain a heart of faith toward God during these long years of struggle. However, I was becoming weary. I had no woman of faith to walk alongside me during these hard times. Oh, I had women in my life, but their relationship with me was distant, no doubt because of my husband. All the scriptures shared with me about "having done all to stand" and "trusting in the Lord" sounded good, but it was the application that eluded me. No one actually showed me how to walk out those truths that sounded so powerful. I was in pain, and nothing was working.

I remembered the countless nights I would stand on my stairs landing, look out into the driveway, and hope the next car would be someone dropping off my husband. I would stand there for hours, crying and praying. One evening the Lord inspired me to read the story of Abigail. It was while reading her story that I began to see a pattern similar to mine. She was married to a man called Nabal, which in the original language literally means "fool." Thus, she was married to a fool who also had no regard for the things of God or those called and chosen by God. Yet, this woman of wisdom and much faith was used by God to save not only her household from certain destruction but she actually saved her husband's life. The real hope that came out of her story was that God killed her husband, Nabal, and she was then married to David, who would be king. Wow! Was there hope in this story for me? Would God destroy the Nabal in my life and give me a king?

I couldn't really conceive how that might happen, but what I did know was that it wouldn't have happened at all without the faith and wisdom of Abigail. What was it about this woman that she still loved, honored, and respected the fool of a man she had married. She had wisdom enough to know not to follow in his ways but follow in the way of faith. She believed that God would use her obedience to Him as just recompense for the ultimate deliverance of her household? This woman, written in scripture, was to become my mentor. I desired and prayed to be like Abigail.

So, for many years she gave me strength to follow in her footsteps, to intercede for my husband and wait on God's redemption. However, the enemy of my soul had one more devastating blow to exact against my faith. My husband had come home really sauced and on something. Probably the PCP he sold. Nonetheless, we got into a very heated argument that almost came to blows! He had picked up an ashtray stand and was aiming it at my head when my sons came in to rescue me. They pulled him away and told me to run. I did run out into the night with my nightgown on and began knocking at my neighbors' doors. They wouldn't answer. I then ran across the street where there was a fire station that was always open. However, when I got to the door, no one was there. How could this be? Someone was always in the station. There was a phone booth outside the station, so I picked it up and began to dial 911. What! How could 911 be busy? I dialed again. Busy? So I dialed the operator. She answered, and I began to tell her exactly what had happened and my concern for my children who were still in the house. She dialed 911 for me, and she too got a busy signal. What was happening? This was like watching a horror movie.

Then, I heard a still, small voice say, "Why are you calling on them for help? Why haven't you called upon me?"

Wow! That statement hit me like a ton of bricks. In my despair and struggle, I ran to men instead of God. How did that happen? I bowed my head and asked the Lord to forgive me for taking matters into my own hands. I asked for His help. However, I did not like His following instruction. I was to return home and submit to my husband. You have got to be kidding. That's not the Lord. That sounds like something the other guy would say. No, I was being instructed to submit myself to my husband.

I crossed the street to return home. I rang the doorbell. He opened the door but would not allow me to enter. He then shut the door, and I sat on the steps and cried. "Father, why? Why is this happening to me?" A few moments later, the door opened, and he ordered me to come in and sit down. He had my kids sitting on the sofa as they watched me being humiliated by the man who just tried to bash my brains out. He told the children to go upstairs to bed. Then he chided me for my actions. I don't even remember what he said; I was so numb. He then told me to go upstairs and wait for him. Oh no! You don't think for one minute I'm going to let you touch me after all that? There was that voice again: "Do not withhold yourself from your husband, and you must apologize for running out of the house."

Honestly! What had I done to deserve this? What? Had I not yielded my life to God's service? Had I not brought my children up to fear God? Had I not sheltered the homeless, fed the hungry, clothed the naked, and even forgiven my husband's infidelity time and time again? Why, Lord? Why? This to me was humility on steroids! Yet, as I cried out to God for strength, He gently reminded me of just how strong I had become. Had this taken place a few years back, I would have attempted to take my life as I had three times before meeting Jesus. The pain was great, but it didn't leave me debilitated to the degree that I was unproductive or unfruitful. Then, He encouraged me with another dream. In this dream, I saw my husband sitting in a dark room with one light just above his head. He was sitting in a chair, and his eyes, mouth, hands, and feet had been duct-taped. He couldn't move or speak. Then, out of the shadows came three demonic figures that would walk around his chair, piercing him with sharp, pointed instruments. As they would jab him, he would flinch in pain, unable to cry out or move. They would stab him over and over again. Then I saw tears falling from under the tape on his eyes. He was in great pain, crying out but unable to free himself or be heard.

The Lord revealed to me that this was the state of my husband. He was in spiritual lockdown, and the enemy was tormenting him. He had no way to free himself, but I had been called and used by God to see many captives set free from the power of the enemy. Yet, here my husband lay beside me, bound by the enemy of his soul, and all I wanted was out! I awakened sobbing and crying. "Lord, forgive me. Please save my husband. No one deserves to be tormented like that, especially not my husband." I discovered that this particular petition I was making for my husband's salvation was unlike the item I wrote down on my list years earlier. You see, what I discovered was the salvation I requested for my husband before had more to do with me and not the glory of the Lord. I wanted my husband to serve me and make me look good to those who ministered with me. The Lord uncovered my very selfish motives for my husband's salvation. It has very little to do with his life being turned over to Jesus. I wanted his life changed and turned over to me. That revelation into my own heart brought me really low. I heard the words from the book of James convicting me when he wrote, "Yet you don't have what you want because you don't ask God for it. And even when you ask, you don't get it because your motives are all wrong—you want only what will give you pleasure." (James 4:2b–3 NLT).

I was broken. Broken indeed by what God showed me was in my heart. How could I go out of the way for so many others and leave my husband behind? Well, after repenting I knew I had to also work on my children's hearts about their stepdad. I asked them to join me in prayer and fasting for my husband. I shared with them what I discovered in my heart and how the Lord showed me that in my husband's weakness, Satan had taken him against his will. I told them that we could not allow him to have their stepdad. I shared that we must forgive and pray for him because he did not know what he was doing. I was not surprised by their answer. They said yes. There were several other days when Satan would use my husband to tempt our faith. He would attempt to spur my older sons to fight. I recall once my oldest son refused to be egged on and said, "I love you, Dad and I know you love me too." My children were going to be given a lesson in humility, right alongside their mom.

What took place next was totally out of my control. Because of the sensitivity of the incident, I will only share that my husband came home one last night under the influence of demon spirits. I knew it because the Holy Spirit had awakened me and instructed me to get up. My husband had come home in the early-morning hours to carry out a diabolical plot that could have taken his freedom away for a very long time. Instead, the Lord permitted me to intervene. The next day, the Lord instructed me to take my children and stay with a friend. We were gone three days, and I was not permitted to respond to my husband's calls or attempts to locate me. On the third day, I was contacted by the police department, who said they had him in custody and it was safe for me and my children to go home. The Lord had made a way for us when there seemed to be no way out of the troubled situation we were in. My children and I had fasted and prayed, not really knowing how the Lord would handle things. However, my husband was now going to be forced to get the care he needed for his addiction.

Yes, God took what the enemy meant for evil and turned it out for our good! He protected us while also protecting my husband. He saw to him getting treatment for his addiction and then began to prepare us for a future reconciliation. We were separated for about three years as the Lord worked on my husband's heart. It was also during this time that he worked on my heart as well.

Although we were separated, the burden of dealing with my husband was not quite over yet. Even while God was working on him while he was away, he still found ways to hurt me. Women that he had befriended while separated now began to call and taunt me into divorcing him. They threatened to come to my house and beat me up simply because I was his wife. Well, this was just too much. He would call and taunt me at work, saying terrible things. He began accusing me, attempting to get money from me. It had begun to be a bit much. I resented his calls, his women, and his refusal to yield himself to God. It had gotten so bad that I would fantasize about my husband getting run over by a Mack truck!

This deadly frame of mind grew and almost caused me to drift toward darkness. My heart ultimately became dark with hatred for my husband. I recall a time the Lord asked me a question. He wanted to know how I would respond to my husband if he were punished and developed cancer. He wanted to know if I could actually watch him slowly succumb to this disease or whether I would be willing to intercede and care for him. The sad truth was that it took me too long to respond. That's how I knew darkness had begun to creep back into my heart. I knew that a true child of God could not approvingly watch someone he or she loves die and waste away. That means there was no love present. It was then that the Lord warned me of His impending correction. The scriptures declare…For whom the Lord loves, He chastens…(Heb. 12:6 NKJ).

Sadly, I didn't care. I had had enough! How long was I to take his mistreatment, his affairs, and his lies! Each year of suffering, my heart was getting darker and darker. Yes! In spite of all the miracles and powerful blessings that I had witnessed in my life, I was not prepared for all this. What I really didn't realize was that it was God permitting me to go through these trials. Even so, I didn't care. I wanted out! No one should have to endure such mistreatment! Especially a child of God. And yes…I knew the Lord had promised to save my husband. However, it was taking much too long. This was too hard and I really didn't deserve this!

The pain of my struggle engulfed me and locked me down in deep darkness. The darkness was so deep that I actually backslid into a life of sin. I hated and resented my husband and "my marriage." Although I called it my marriage, I didn't realize that marriage belonged to God. It was a gift given to a man and a woman to bring glory and honor to His name and bring forth righteous seed into the earth. However, my marriage was a failure, and my husband's treatment of me was just much more than I could bear.

As far as I was concerned, I had done everything I was supposed to do, serving God and working two and sometimes three jobs to keep us afloat. But this Nabal of a man was taking me through literal hell, and it wasn't fair! I was oblivious to the fact that I was being played by the enemy of my soul, again. He was weaving a diabolic plot against me to draw me away from my Father and my God. He had found something of himself in me and begun to set up a stronghold around it. The scripture says that when Jesus knew Satan was coming, He said, "For the prince of this world cometh, and hath nothing in me" (John 14:30). Sad to say, that was not my claim to fame. When Satan came to sift me, he found something of himself to build upon. My concern for my own well-being and need had begun to overshadow and dismiss my husband's need for a believing wife to stand and fight for him.

The enemy knew and took full advantage of my pain and grief. What he did was to offer me something seemingly better. By this seemingly better thing he offered, I was lured into a web of adultery that ultimately shook the very core of my faith. You see, I had prided myself in keeping myself pure in the area of sexual sin. I thought of it as the hallmark of my testimony before God, not realizing that it was the state of my heart that had been compromised by pride and works. I took pride in my ability to resist sexual temptation and flirtation, and to do great works, thinking I had done it for the sake of the kingdom. I was fooled into thinking that my works would, in themselves, bring about the blessings and favor of God I so desired. However, I was about to find out that I was terribly wrong.

Well, what happened was—I fell. That's right! Yes...this tongue talking, devil stalking, sanctified woman of God fell flat on her face. After all the miracles and wonders the Lord had revealed to me, I allowed my enemy to play me. He literally pulled the dark wool, woven by my circumstances, over my eyes, and I ultimately began to seek out provision for my flesh. Do you know there is a warning against that? "But put on Christ, and make no plans to satisfy the fleshly desires" (Rom. 13:14). But, I wanted better for myself and my children! I wanted a man who would love me, respect me, and provide for me. You see, this segment of my journey just wasn't doing me any good. I began to long for the leeks and garlic of life. I did not see Jesus as a "present help" for me. I needed something more tangible, and I needed it right then!

After my fall things only got worse. The man I thought would be my knight in shining armor became another terrible burden and albatross around my neck, not to mention that I had caused this man to sin with my actions. What in the world was I thinking! Once I came to realize the hopelessness of such an affair, I attempted to end it, only to be faced with my lover's threats of suicide. Lord, what had I gotten myself into? It was like jumping out of the frying pan into the fire all over again! Here I was with a drug-addicted, delinquent husband and now a suicidal lover. It had become so deeply dark that even I began contemplating suicide. Yes, with all that I had experienced with my Father, I, like Israel, began longing for Egypt. Although I had been fed with manna from on high, the fattening meat of quail, and had watched God bring water out of a rock, I still was not satisfied. I was in deep trouble, and only God could bring me out. I remember in my deepest despair crying out to God and saying, "Father, unless you come after me, I don't think I can make it."

But God, who is rich in mercy, spoke a word of hope into my spirit. He said, "Nadine, I am the One who began this work in you, and I am the one Who will finish it! (Phil. 1:6). Although I was in a backslidden state, I didn't want to stay there. I knew that it would mean spiritual suicide for me. But my flesh had gained strength and was crying out for relief. I left the church, stopped teaching the Word, and stopped serving in all capacities because of the darkness in my heart. I felt as if I was too far gone and had wandered so far from God. Then, God sent an angel. One Saturday a very close woman of God came and literally told me I was going to church with her. I looked at her like she was crazy because her tone was quite strong. She literally told me I was going to get my butt up and I was going with her to church. I fussed and argued, but she won. She took me to a Jewish service in Rockville, Maryland. I wasn't feeling it. I wanted to go home. However, as the music began to play and a company of women praise dancers began to dance, waving their flags in the air, it gave me a strong sense of the presence of the Lord. I actually began to feel the Holy Spirit hover over the deep darkness of my heart. It was quite powerful. Then, the pastor or speaker stepped out to speak and said these words, "I cannot bring the message because there is someone here in the audience who is a minister for Christ and has fallen and thinks God has forsaken them. Well," he said, "the Lord wants me to let you know that as He left the ninety-nine to go after the one, He is coming after you, to restore you unto Himself!"

Yes! My loving and merciful Father used those terms—"coming after you." Now how wild was that! Only God and I knew of the conversation we had about my needing Him to come after me. There was no way this man knew of that conversation except the Holy Spirit revealed it to him. The Father wanted me to know that not only did He hear my cry but that He was going to come after me...again!

Well, you should know my MO by now...I fell down on my knees into a sobbing heap, just as I had that first morning He showed up in my bedroom, and I began to weep cleansing tears of joy. Wow! The Lord was making it clear once again that He and He alone is the Lord God Almighty and that besides Him there is none other! His love for me was greater than my sin. He came and rescued me; He picked me up also out of the pit, out of the miry clay, and set my feet upon a rock! That Rock is Jesus Christ, my Savior.

So, yes—the righteous may fall, but by the love and grace of an almighty God, we can get back up! And yes...there will be those in the church who will write you off after your first infraction and crucify you upon your second. But, beloved, that's them. That is not how our Father operates. As I learned firsthand, we may have very little capacity for extending to others the same grace that God has dealt to us. There are even some who may gloat at your demise with the pointing of the finger and their proclamations of impending doom. Not the Father. He has provided His Son to deal with our sin. And He did, once and for all. Just as you wouldn't spank an eleven-month-old who falls while taking their first steps, your heavenly Father doesn't condemn your missteps. Grace dealt with our indiscretions on the cross. He wants us to learn to walk by faith but it won't happen overnight. It is a journey and a process. But, beloved, don't wait too long. Learn from your missteps and mistakes. Get back up, and press your way onto the path the Lord has set for you. "The righteous falls seven times, and gets back up" (Prov. 24:16).

As I mentioned earlier, the fight has been rigged in our favor. God has provided victory for all of His children who will just believe Him. Beloved, God is not a man, that He would lie to us. Nor is He the son of men, to have to change His mind. But everything that He has promised, He is well able to perform!—that's my paraphrase of Numbers 23:19. His word declares, "*'I know the plans I have for you,' declares the Lord, 'plans to prosper you and not to harm you, plans to give you hope and a future'*" (*Jeremiah 29:11 NIV*).

Psalm 18:4–18 is a psalm of David that comforted me.

The ropes of death entangled me; floods of destruction swept over me. The grave wrapped its ropes around me; death laid a trap in my path. But in my distress I cried out to the Lord; yes, I prayed to my God for help. He heard me from his sanctuary; my cry to him reached his ears. Then the earth quaked and trembled. The foundations of the mountains shook; they quaked because of his anger. Smoke poured from his nostrils; fierce flames leaped from his mouth. Glowing coals blazed forth from him. He opened the heavens and came down; dark storm clouds were beneath his feet. Mounted on a mighty angelic being, he flew, soaring on the wings of the wind. He shrouded himself in darkness, veiling his approach with dark rain clouds. Thick clouds shielded the brightness around him and rained down hail and burning coals. The Lord thundered from heaven; the voice of the Most High resounded amid the hail and burning coals. He shot his arrows and scattered his enemies; great bolts of lightning flashed, and they were confused. Then at your command, O Lord, at the blast of your breath, the bottom of the sea could be seen, and the foundations of the earth were laid bare. He reached down from heaven and rescued me; he drew me out of deep waters. He rescued me from my powerful enemies, from those who hated me and were too strong for me. They attacked me at a moment when I was in distress, but the Lord supported me. He led me to a place of safety; he rescued me because he delights in me.

5

O YE OF LITTLE FAITH

And immediately Jesus stretched forth his hand,
and caught him, and said unto him, O thou
of little faith, wherefore didst thou doubt?

—Matthew 14:31 (KJV)

I believe that Faith was the ultimate key ingredient that catapulted me forward into this part of my uncertain journey as a born-again child of God. There is just no way my husband and I would be together today except for the faith the Father so graciously bestowed upon me. There were many prayers for which I was going to need answers, and faith was going to be necessary in order for me to receive the answers I desired.

I have witnessed many new births that have tragically become spiritual stillbirths. No further life or divine activity detectable. I believe it is because their faith never grew beyond the moment of their decision to surrender to Jesus. I believe that when Jesus told his disciples to tarry in Jerusalem and wait for the promised Comforter, He knew there would be no way for them to sustain their lifestyle of commitment to Him and His Word without faith and the indwelling power of the Holy Spirit. Such was my case. Such as it is with every born-again believer. Upon accepting Jesus as my Lord and Savior, scripture teaches that it is at that moment that the Holy Spirit baptized us into the body of Christ. This, I believe, is when life's uncertain journey took a turn for the better. This spiritual operation of God is not visible to the naked eye. It's done in the spirit realm and is conducted by the Spirit of God. However, there was a subsequent spiritual operation that needed to take place. I was going to need that same Holy Spirit that baptized me into the body of Christ to also indwell me, and that was going to take faith. There were going to be spiritual encounters that would require more than human ability to overcome. I had no idea the level of spiritual warfare I would be engaged in, warfare that could only be won by faith in the power of God working in and through me by His indwelling Holy Spirit. I would often tell women that had it not been for God's provision of faith, faith to believe Him for some rather impossible things, and the indwelling presence of the Holy Spirit, I would probably be a bitter, cynical old divorcee today. In order for me to be victorious in this new life, I needed the God kind of faith (Mark 11:23) accompanied by the indwelling power of the Holy Ghost. I actually shudder to think that my life would not look like it does now had it not been for God's mercy and most importantly faith in the Father by the Holy Spirit's help. I know that even the ability to wait on the Lord was not of human origin. It had to come from the Lord. I know because in my flesh I wanted to jump ship. There was mutiny on board in my house, and I couldn't handle it. God kept me during those dark days. He had a plan and a purpose not only for me but for my husband. God provided what I needed. But had He not been the source of my faith and strength, someone else would be enjoying my husband and the fruit of my agonizing labor suffered while waiting on the manifestation of the promise. That's right! I would be watching him driving around life with another woman who would reap the benefit of my inability to trust and wait on God. Thank you, Lord!

Beloved, one of the greatest things I believe I learned through this phase of my journey was never to judge a thing before it's time (1 Cor. 4:5). You see, I easily could have accepted what I "saw" in my husband's actions and behaviors as the final product of who he was to become. But the Lord provided me more grace. He used a simple cockroach crawling across my kitchen floor to teach me something of His infinite power. The Father knew how best to get His point across to me. He would use visuals (dreams and visions). I learn better by watching and He knew that. As my loving Father, He would use this as His means of teaching me things.

So, one night while waiting for my husband to come home, I was pacing the floor, seething with anger. I couldn't wait until he got home to light into him for his late-night shenanigans. I saw a cock-roach crawl from under the kitchen cabinet, headed toward my liv-ing room. However, I could see that there was an object that would prevent him from scurrying into the living room. I recall mentioning to myself that the minute he got to that broom it would be over for him. I knew this because I was at a visual advantage high above it. I could see the path it was taking and the broom that was in its way. As I watched this roach scurrying across the floor, I heard, "I am the Lord Who sits high and looks low, and I see the end from the beginning. Nothing is outside my purview. You look upon your hus-band with finite vision that is limited and obscured by time. I see the end from the beginning, and your husband, who you see today as a heathen and unsaved, I see him today saved and my man of God. Be careful not to judge a thing before it is time. Do not condemn what I have blessed, for I have declared that every tongue that rises up in judgment shall be condemned. You dare judge my man of God out of your finite limited vision of Him. Beloved, do not err!"

I learned a valuable lesson watching that little cockroach that night. I repented for judging my husband. I was thankful because the Lord loved me so much that He revealed this valuable truth to me so that I would trust Him even more. Today, I am still thankful because I now see the man of God He saw back then when I was call-ing him everything but a child of God. Although I am forgiven, I will have to give an account for those things I spoke against my husband. But I thank God for the warning so that I wouldn't go forth judging him or anyone else based upon my finite, limited vision of things. Beloved, God knows the end of the story. We can never look upon someone today who may be lost as eternally lost. Tomorrow that same person, unknown to us, could accept Jesus as Lord of their lives while we would go on in ignorance, condemning that person.

Yes, there were many years of hurt, anxiety, and pain as I waited on the manifestation of God's promise to save my husband. And, as I shared in the previous chapter, I didn't handle it very well at all. In spite of the countless miracles and provisions the Lord gave to confirm His presence and power in my life, the pain I was experiencing was just excruciating. It was just too much, or so I told myself. Today I understand that "the sufferings of this present time are not worthy to be compared with the glory which was to be revealed in me" (Rom. 8:18). The pain distracted and blinded me to the truth that I had been called to this, just as I had been called to see miracles and power from on high! While I was yet in my struggle, it just didn't really sink in that "Christ also suffered for me, leaving me an example, that I should follow in His steps (1 Pet. 2:21). Nor was I able to compare what I was called to endure to be anywhere near as difficult as what Jesus had suffered for me. Hebrews 12:4 confirmed to me that my pain and struggle did not require the shedding of my blood or the piercing of my body as it had my Lord.

I praise God that I am able to share my struggle with you today. They say that hindsight is twenty-twenty. Well, if that be so, here is your opportunity to get ahead of the game by learning that God is able to work all things together for your good because He loves us. He takes the good, the bad, and the ugly and makes it into something wonderful. But we have to do this thing His way. We must realize that our Father does have a plan and a purpose for our lives. When we said yes to Him, we actually said, "Do with my life as you please, Lord. I want to live for you." No one actually explains that to us when they are running off all the wonderful things salvation brings. They don't tell us Jesus required that we count the cost before following Him (Luke 14:26-33). There is a cost, beloved! Your life as you knew it must end. You must be willing to surrender it all—family, fame, and fortune all go onto the altar as you surrender your life to Christ (Luke 14:26–33). As I have said before, all that I endured I would do again. Yes, I would. There is nothing more wonderful than experiencing the power and blessings God has in store for everyone who surrenders him- or herself into His care. The devil wants us to see life his way. Jesus says, "See life my way because I am the Way, the Truth, and the Life!"

Getting back to my struggle, I had become so frustrated waiting on God to deliver this man. It seemed like the more I prayed, the worse he would get. Ultimately, I felt it necessary to take matters into my own hands, and so I began to dig my own cistern. I found myself written in the prophecy of Jeremiah, committing two evils, forsaking God and digging out my own provisional cistern (Jer. 2:12–13). I needed immediate intervention because I had had enough! I wanted out!

But, God! There it was again! Every time I would hear those words quoted, I would get teary-eyed. Actually, I had many But, God" moments in my life. However, after failing so miserably in my faith and commitment to my Father, I was a prime candidate for Satan's trickery. He went all out to ultimately annihilate of my faith and render me chained and shackled back into his domain of darkness. It was his plan to steal my joy, kill my faith, and destroy my life.

However, as I shared earlier, my Father came after me. He brought me back to my senses as He did King Nebuchadnezzar. God had permitted this man to roam around like an animal when he refused to surrender himself. However, at the appointed time, which I believe is when he finally surrendered, the Lord granted his senses to return to him (Dan. 4:33–34). Once the Lord restored me and allowed me to return to ministry, I was angry at the devil for tricking me. I was determined to stand and fight for my husband's life. He was in brutal bondage and needed someone to stand in the gap for him. I was his wife, so who best to go to battle for what was mine? I resolved to love, intercede, and care for my husband and fight the good fight of faith. It would mean being willing to die to my own needs as a wife. It would mean not wearing my emotions on my sleeve, getting upset over things I had no power to change, but trusting in the one Who could. It meant biting my tongue when I wanted to preach him a good sermon and trusting the Lord to speak to his heart. It was not my place to teach my husband; I had to learn that he was a job for Jesus! What I did know is I had to treat him as God had revealed, a man of God. No, he wasn't acting like it. He wasn't talking like a man of God. However, I needed to obey God based on what I was told, not what I saw. Slowly but surely, the Father began to orchestrate things in our lives that would lead to my husband's salvation. There would still be some fierce battles to fight; however, God provided everything we needed to endure.

6

ENDURING THE SIFTING OF SATAN

*Satan hath desired to have you, that he may sift you as
wheat: But I have prayed for thee, that thy faith fail not:
and when thou art converted, strengthen thy brethren.*

—Luke 22:31–32

It is sad that the knowledge of the Father's love for us has been
obscured by an enemy who does not want it known. We have entered life with either no knowledge of God or a false impression
of Him. This lack of knowledge has violently impacted the lives of
many. Yet our heavenly Father goes to great lengths to reach us with
the Truth. His Truth is that we belong to Him and He truly loves us
very much. He created us and sent us into the earth's realm with a
mission and a purpose—to do His will and to declare His name to
the world! Unfortunately we, like Adam and Eve, were sidetracked,
hoodwinked, and bamboozled. We were hijacked and sold into slav-
ery to a world's system and ideology orchestrated by none other
than Satan himself. You see, Satan is our Father's enemy. He is also
our enemy, by virtue of our relationship to the Father. This enemy
does not want any of the purposes of God to be fulfilled because
it would mean his own demise and dethronement over the earth's
realm and its inhabitants. Satan, also known as Lucifer, is real. I

know you've heard of him but may have, like many others, relegated him also to be just a fairy tale. Believe me, he is no fairy tale (Isa. 14:12–15).

Satan devised a diabolic plot to overthrow the kingdom of God, which was to be established here on earth. Many of us were taught as children to pray "Thy kingdom come, Thy will be done on earth as it is in heaven" (Matt. 6:10). However, we are sometimes oblivious to the fact that there are evil forces working against that happening.

Beloved, know this: God is faithful! He came up with the plan for our redemption, as well as our enemy's demise. It will most certainly happen, in God's timing. But until that day, our Father has provided us with everything we need to stand, fight, conquer, and live victoriously in the midst of a world filled with darkness, evil, injustice, and pain (2 Pet. 1:3). Yes beloved, we are in the middle of a great battle against the forces of darkness that have been marked for destruction. Yet our King and Sovereign Lord reigns in the heavenlies and in the hearts and minds of His children and has declared that no weapon formed against us shall prosper (Isa. 54:17)! When our Savior rose from the grave, He proclaimed that "all power in heaven and earth has been given unto me" (Matt. 28:18–19)." He then added, "Therefore, go and make disciples of all nations." Jesus made it possible for us to go forth without fear, guilt, or condemnation. He freed us from servitude to Satan, to receive the blessings of an eternal and abundant life, now in this time! Satan, the god of this world, no longer has a right to you, your family, your health, or your finances. He no longer has power or authority over those who have entrusted themselves to the care of Jesus Christ, our Savior. We have been given the victory; it's now time for us to walk in it (Col. 2:13–15).

Beloved, the Lord has chosen and equipped us to wage warfare and overthrow the kingdom of darkness. We do this by the blood of the Lamb and the word of our testimony (Rev. 12:11). He created you for Himself! He has a divine plan and purpose for your life! You may be ignorant to this truth now, as even I was. It may not even register that God knows you are around. Well…He does! He knows because He set you in this earthly realm with a purpose. *His* purpose! That you and I may show forth the reality of His glory! He will provide the signs and wonders. He will also make you to become an effective witness for Him. He imparts His Holy Spirit to give us the power and ability to represent Him well. Satan knows this and would rather keep this truth hidden from you. The scripture actually says that "Satan, who is the god of this world, has blinded the minds of those who don't believe. They are unable to see the glorious light of the Good News. They don't understand this message about the glory of Christ, who is the exact likeness of God" (2 Cor. 4:4).

Please, don't let this news discourage or demean you into thinking it means that you are unworthy to experience the knowledge and blessings the Father has for you. Not at all! Actually, we are in good company. Even the great apostle Paul succumbed to the same demonic blindness. He said in 1 Timothy 1:12–14, "I thank Christ Jesus our Lord, who has given me strength, that he considered me trustworthy, appointing me to his service. Even though I was once a blasphemer and a persecutor and a violent man, I was shown mercy because I acted in ignorance and unbelief. The grace of our Lord was poured out on me abundantly, along with the faith and love that are in Christ Jesus." Did you hear that? Paul wrote many of the New Testament epistles, yet he too was duped by the enemy. He was sidetracked just like I was (Phil. 3:4–9). He, like many others, was attempting to keep the laws of Moses, not realizing that no human being could accomplish that. He learned once He met Jesus that knowing Him was much more powerful than trying to keep the law. He learned that Jesus never wanted his works and efforts, He wanted him.

Beloved, God created you, and He wants you! He doesn't want works and human effort. He desires to have a real relationship with you. He has paved the way for you to turn away from this world as you know it and desires that you turn to the Father. The innocent blood of Jesus Christ has already been shed for your sinful and rebellious heart. Jesus is God's plan to defeat Satan's hold over your life. He was sent to open the eyes of the blind and to set at liberty those of us held captive by Satan's lies (Isa. 61:1–3). The scriptures say "that God was in Christ, reconciling the world unto himself, not imputing their trespasses unto them (2 Cor. 5:19a). He went to great lengths to get us back, beloved! Even to giving up the life of His own Son, who never once committed sin, never once denied Him, never once disobeyed Him. There was no reason for Christ to die except to please His Father by taking upon Himself the punishment we deserved so that we could have relationship with the Father. Jesus was the God/Man who did what Adam could not do. He fulfilled the plan of God by defeating His enemy and ours—Satan! Jesus is our Savior! Satan has no more power to deceive or defeat us as long as we enter into a saving relationship with Jesus. Once we are in His hands, no thing and no one can pluck us out! The scripture says, "Therefore there is now no condemnation [no guilty verdict, no punishment] for those who are in Christ Jesus [who believe in Him as personal Lord and Savior]. For the law of the Spirit of life [which is] in Christ Jesus [the law of our new being] has set you free from the law of sin and of death. For what the Law could not do [that is, overcome sin and remove its penalty, its power] being weakened by the flesh [man's nature without the Holy Spirit], God did: He sent His own Son in the likeness of sinful humanity as an offering for sin. And He condemned sin in the flesh [subdued it and overcame it in the person of His own Son], so that the [righteous and just] requirement of the Law might be fulfilled in us who do not live our lives in the ways of the flesh [guided by worldliness and our sinful nature], but [live our lives] in the ways of the Spirit [guided by His power]" (Rom. 8:1–4).

It goes on to say, "What then shall we say to all these things? If God is for us, who can be [successful] against us? He Who did not spare [even] His own Son, but gave Him up for us all, how will He not also, along with Him, graciously give us all things? Who will bring any charge against God's elect (His chosen ones)? It is God Who justifies us [declaring us blameless and putting us in a right relationship with Himself]. Who is the one who condemns us? Christ Jesus is the One who died [to pay our penalty], and more *than that*, Who was raised [from the dead], and Who is at the right hand of God interceding [with the Father] for us. Who shall ever separate us from the love of [d]Christ? Will tribulation, or distress, or persecution, or famine, or nakedness, or danger, or sword? Just as it is written *and* forever remains written, "For Your sake we are put to death all day long; we are regarded as sheep for the slaughter." Yet in all these things we are more than conquerors *and* gain an overwhelming victory through Him who loved us [so much that He died for us]. For I am convinced [and continue to be convinced—beyond any doubt] that neither death, nor life, nor angels, nor principalities, nor things present *and* threatening, nor things to come, nor powers, nor height, nor depth, nor any other created thing, will be able to separate us from the [unlimited] love of God, which is in Christ Jesus our Lord" (Rom. 8:32–39).

I have been blessed to have God's glorious grace poured out upon me and my story bears witness to how all these promises played themselves out in my life. It is why I trust wholeheartedly in God's Word! They are Spirit, and they are Life! They were given to guide and direct our lives, but we have relegated them to children stories and fairy tales. Beloved, study and believe God's Word! I will proclaim His Word, His goodness, and His glory wherever I go! The scripture says, "God made His ways known unto Moses...but His acts to the children of Israel" (Ps. 103:7). God wants you to know His ways and to behold His mighty acts!

Now, I would like for you to hear my husband's side of this testimony. A testimony of one is no testimony at all without a witness. My husband is not only that witness but the evidence of what God can and will do if we would only believe!

7

MY HUSBAND'S TESTIMONY

Amazing grace, how sweet the sound, that
saved a wretch like me. I once was lost, but
now I'm found; was blind but now I see.

— "Amazing Grace," by John Newton

I was born totally blind in Waycross, Georgia, in 1949, and long before I met my wife, I was one man who lived three different lives. My family moved to a small town called Aliquippa, Pennsylvania. I think I was about three months old, so of course I don't remember anything about life in Waycross, Georgia. We lived in an undeveloped area in the woods of Pennsylvania, where yelling across the way was how we communicated. It was quite normal. But if you wanted to get a word to someone, you would simply holler (Hey!) to the first person you saw and asked them to call whomever you were trying to reach. That person then would yell to the next person, and so on. This could go on and on, back and forth for quite some miles, night or day. Of course, everybody knew your business. This area in Aliquippa where I grew up was called the hollow.

Because everybody knew everybody, strangers had a hard way to go. I lived deep in the hollow up in the woods where nobody came unless you were invited. Most of the food we ate we grew or raised.

For example, we had our own garden, raised pigs and chickens, and had plenty of fruit trees. Before you ask, yes—my dad made moonshine, home-brew, and wine.

People up in the hood (the hollow) would come up and buy these drinks from my dad.

As a little boy, I would stray away from home a lot because no one ever watched me. I don't think it mattered much because there was really nowhere to go. When I was gone too long, I heard the yelling start: "John Lee! Where is John Lee?" Sometimes I would go down the hill to try to find friends. I loved those days.

I was named after my uncle who worked in the steel mill where most of the people worked. He was a foreman. That was a big job during those days. His boss was a Sicilian who also had a blind son about my age. Sometimes, my uncle took me with him to visit with the son of his boss. We became best friends. Sometimes he would visit at my house, and sometimes I would be dropped off at his house. I had a brother who was a bully, and he used to be so angry all the time because he had to watch out for me. He could not have much fun because of me. That made him very angry, and when my friend would come to visit me, that meant my brother would have to watch out for both of us. Having to watch out for two blind kids was no fun for him. We were only five or six years old, and my brother was only one year older, so he really didn't know how to watch anyone, let alone watch out for us.

My friend's dad decided to send him to blind school, and he also asked my uncle if he wanted me to attend. They asked my mom, and she said yes. I don't think she really cared because I was out of her hair, and that was all she really needed.

Before I went to blind school, I had to be about six or seven because I remember my mom trying to get me into regular school. But I couldn't see anything, so I stayed in trouble because I always asked a lot of questions and disturbed the class.

It isn't that I was smarter than the other kids; I just could not see what the teacher was writing on the chalkboard, so I asked questions. I remember the teacher saying, "Can't you see?" I felt very bad because when the teacher asked that question, I wouldn't answer. Because I couldn't see, everyone would laugh at me. My brother was in the same room, and when the kids laughed at me, he did too. The teacher, my brother, and the kids would laugh at me. They would also call me names. Names like four eyes, blind bat, and names I can't say because they were too filthy. The teacher would often send me to the office, and the principal would send me home by myself. And I always got lost. But God was with me even then.

This would happen just about every day I went to school. A couple of the old drunks used to always help me get to the road I lived on because everyone knew everyone. When I was leaving school, the yelling started: "John Lee is out of school!" All the way until I got to the road home.

I never cared about the teasing or anything. I don't know why, but I didn't care. I did, however, feel bad for my brother because they teased him about me. There were two other guys besides me and my brother who grew up on that road. The two other guys seemed to love me more than my brother because they did not have to take care of me, but they did. They shared everything with me without asking for anything in return. So, I had three good friends. We formed a club called the four aces. A couple of them always argued over who was the ace of hearts or the ace of spades. We had no heroes and didn't really know what holidays really meant. We did know that once a year we got one toy each. Broke or not, we were thankful. I don't remember much after that of the neighborhood because I went off to blind school.

I don't know what grade I started school, but what I do know is that I went to school all year around, and I loved that. I would come home about two or three times a year. I would see my bully brother. It was OK because he did not know that blind school was teaching me self-defense. Good for me, bad for him. His bullying days were over. I never picked a fight, but I finished them.

Every time I came home, I had to fight with my brother just because my mother had said for him take care of me. I did feel bad for him. He did not bring me into this world, he was not my dad, and he had no fun when I came home. Before you pass judgment on my mom for not being a good mom, know that she was not raised by her mom. Many men took advantage of her, and no one was around to help her. She was beaten by many men and had many kids. Yes, my dad also beat my mom many times before he died. I never got to know my dad. The dad I did know was my stepdad, and he knew and loved the Lord.

He was the one who took care of me without asking for anything in return. The only other person who I know who loved the Lord in my family was my older sister. I would always hear her praying at night, even before I went to blind school, and when I sometimes came home to visit, she had not changed. She still would be praying every night. "Lord," she would say, "help me and help my brothers and sisters, and forgive us for trespassing against you." I knew she was talking to the Lord because sometimes I would hear the Lord talking to me. The first thing I remember the Lord telling me was, "If the wind don't blow, don't go." That meant that if the wind was blowing in my face, then I could go. I would listen to everything around me, and if something was blocking the sound, that meant there was something in front of me or beside me, so I would stop. If the wind doesn't blow, don't go.

After I broke my brother's arm in a fight, my friends started calling me Juda Mass. My friend's cousin could not say my nickname because of a speech impediment, so he called me Juice. Nobody would pick at me anymore or call me a name to my face. Most people stopped picking on me. I thought it was neat to have a cool nickname.

As I mentioned, I would only come home about two or three times a year. Over about nine or ten years, my blind friend and I became very close, and I got another nickname at blind school: Curly. At the blind school, I met some wonderful friends and had a great mentor. One of my friends became a great jazz musician who played the saxophone. My mentor at blind school did not play. He was my martial-arts instructor. He was very serious, and his words encouraged me to become independently able to take care of myself. He said when I fall down, get up and don't cry. He said, "When you are little, people love you and take care of you, but when you become a teenager, they might help you a little, but when you get older, everybody will stay away from you, so get ready now." He taught me to learn the elements because they are our friends. We can trust them. They don't come from humanity but from God. He was my mentor from the time I started blind school to the time I left. He said to me on parting that I was not his best student nor his worst. He said, "I love you, I will miss you, and go with God."

Once when I was home visiting my family, one of my cousins, who is now deceased, was playing outside our house with me, and he accidentally hit me in the head on my eyebrow with a metal duck used for a bookend. I fell down a twenty-foot hill filled with briar bushes. Long sharp needles went into my eyes and head. My cousin screamed for help. Frightened, he said, "I was just playing, and I accidentally hit him with the duck."

Then I heard the yelling. "Oh, my baby!" Somebody came and got me and took me to my grandma. She said, "He's blind anyway, so these needles can't hurt his eyes. I'll take them out and rap his head up to stop the bleeding." She put spider webs all around my head under a dirty cloth because she had to stop the bleeding. I went back to school a couple days later, and my house parents there took me to the doctor, changed my bandages, and gave me something for pain. I think I had bandages on for at least three or four months before they removed them.

You would think the day they removed them should've been one of the best days of my life, but it was the worst. That was the day I first began to see things out of my eyes. Just as in the Bible, what I saw looked like trees moving around. The trees were actually the doctor's hands moving in the front of my face. The doctor asked me why I grabbed his hand, and I said, "I see something moving in front of me." The doctor said to do it again, so I did it again. That was the first time I remember seeing anything. For about another year, my sight became clearer and clearer, up to the point that I could see colors. I had to have someone explain to me what the colors were. My doctor said that because I had a disease in my eyes and glaucoma that my eyes would begin to deteriorate again, so I should not depend on them for my sight but continue to read braille. My mentor told me that I should learn to read words and understand what letters meant. One of my eyes could see light, but only one of them could see words. I found out when I tried to look at what I saw, I would get severe headaches. So I began to glance at things but not try to look directly at them.

The doctors were amazed at my sight recovery because I was born blind and had never seen anything. But now this is why I said it was the worst day for me. I was told that I should try to go to public school. I remembered the teasing I had to endure during that time, and I said to myself, "No way." I was in the tenth grade when I left blind school and started public school. The public schools put me in the ninth grade because I couldn't see very well. They would put me in the front of the classroom. However, I was smarter than most of the students in the class, so when the teacher asked questions, I would not only answer the questions but also explain to her where she was wrong. That didn't go too well with the teacher because the students began to laugh at her. So they put me in the back of the classroom with the bad guys, and they became my friends. They liked me because I would give them the answers to the tests. The teacher didn't care because most of the bad guys were football players, and most of them knew my family. I really did not like these guys because they began to pick on the other kids who were not as popular or had a disability. The number-one bully was my brother. My teacher sent me a tenth-grade teacher to see if I could do the grade work. The work was easy, so they sent me on to the eleventh-grade teacher to see if I could do that work. It was easy too, so they sent me to the twelfth-grade teacher, and I aced the test they take for graduation. All this happened within a six-month time period. So the teachers and the principal asked my mom to take me to Beaver County Community College and see how I tested. I ended up a junior at Beaver County Community College that same year. I was about sixteen years old.

When I got some of my sight, I wanted to know everything about everything. I wanted to know about women, drinking, and taking drugs. I lived at home with my mom, but I still tried everything. I got a terrible reputation as being really bold, cold, and mean. On my seventeenth birthday, I asked God to let me enjoy the world for one more year, and when I was eighteen, I would turn my life over to Him. But when I became eighteen, I asked him to allow me to enjoy the world till I was twenty-one. Unfortunately, by that time I had about ten kids, became a drug abuser, and developed a reputation as a pimp. I cared about nothing and nobody. I was very angry because there were no jobs for the partially blind, and everybody knew I couldn't see very well. Every good job in that community was either steel-mill, foundry, or factory work. I couldn't pass any equipment-use test. They all liked me but could not hire me because I would possibly hurt myself or someone else. So I was what you might call an educated fool. I even gave myself the nickname the devil's son.

After school I began to travel by myself. I said to myself, "I'm going to visit Motown in Detroit, Michigan, and I'll become the biggest pimp in the world. I had watched many guys in my town use women and watched women use men. I knew how to use them both against each other. I knew both of them had one thing in common—greed. But I was the greediest of them all. I could lie better, cheat, scheme, and connive them into doing what I wanted them to do. So I took my show on the road. But I needed some money to front with. So I tricked one of the drug dealers out of some marijuana, sold it back to him, and then left town. When he figured out what I had done, I threatened to tell the police on him. Of course, the street code is "snitches get stitches." But now he was no longer dealing with Juice; he was dealing with the devil's son. I had places to go and a short time to get there.

A friend of mine made it to New York. He lived in Harlem, and so he said he was going home to visit his family because things had gotten hot. I hitched a ride with him in a stolen car. By the time we got there, he did it to "23 skidoo." That meant "stay here, and I'll be back." But he didn't know that when he said to stay there, when he went in the store, I left before he did. With his bags and everything in them. I didn't tell him anything. I was on my way to claim my fame, and he was just dead luggage. Things got hot really quickly in New York, looking for a big name; I ran into big-name people. I lived on 125th and 9th Avenues in New York City, right smack dab in the middle of trouble. I loved it.

I found a couple of used and abused weak-minded women, and I used my little bit of drugs to get them to work for me. That lasted only a little while until their old pimp saw them on the street and put them back to work. He had a gang. I was by myself, so it was time to go. Nothing wrong with it; that's just the way of the street. So, I was off to the next move, Cleveland Ohio. I stayed about two weeks, then got on the bus to Chicago, the Windy City. It was easy to blend in because everybody hated everybody. But I could only stay a little while in the Windy City. It was hot there, and I am not talking about the weather. One of the guys' mothers used to be a prostitute. I met her one night and talked her into working for me. This only lasted a couple weeks. She was introducing me to a lot of old prostitutes who still wanted to do the game. That was great for me at the time. But brother man found out that his mama was my number-one girl and wanted to shoot me. I knew then it was time to go. Took my money and a couple of the girls, got on the bus, and went to Detroit, Michigan. My track went from Detroit (never made it to Motown), New York, and Cleveland, then I went out to Los Angeles, California. I made a little money. I was stylin' and profilin', moving from state to state. My lifestyle got the eye of the police. I left Detroit and went to DC.

I got to DC late '60s, early '70s. I had my ladies working around Maryland and Virginia, making me money left and right. I had a couple of them working on the strip joint on Fourteenth Street in DC. Life was good. They had a new mayor who liked prostitutes and thought he was cool. He also had a bad drug problem. I let my girls have their way with him. My reputation grew, and I had some of the best marijuana in the DC metropolitan area. I didn't have a lot, but I had the best in the area. I only sold to certain people, and I only sold a little bit at a time. I made a lot of money. After a while, I only had one or two girls left. It was OK; it was time to change my stock anyway. I moved in with my sister and actually got a part-time job moving furniture. I started to meet women who actually had jobs.

They were really easy to train to take care of me. But I couldn't have them continue to come to my sister's house all times of the night and day. It was like a revolving door. One came in the front door and sat in the living room and another one would be in the basement and the other one left by the back door. This went on for about two years. I weeded troublemakers out and just kept a couple who were really meeting my needs and especially my wants. Any woman who fell in love had to go. One day a customer stopped by to buy some weed. She was a good customer because she brought me good business by spreading the word about my goods. One day she came over with her best friend, who ultimately became my wife. She was cool, but she was different too. She told me she was married but separated. That was OK. Her husband was a woman beater, and I hated woman beaters. She began coming by rather frequently by herself. When I asked about her husband, she said she didn't care about him and wasn't afraid of him. She eventually ran all my girls away. She broke all of my pimp rules. Don't get it wrong; I was not her pimp. She was too strong willed for that. However, she cared about me, unlike the other women in my life. She also had three little kids, who I just fell in love with.

My stepdad raised me, and I loved what my dad did for me and wanted to be like him. One day Nadine decided she wanted to move away from her husband. Because of his physical abuse toward her and shooting her brother, he was ordered by the courts to stay away from her. However, he paid her rent out of guilt. Although the courts demanded he stay away, she would allow him to visit with the children. However, this was becoming a problem, as he began to demand to come over or he would stop paying her rent. She was tired of it and wanted to move in to her own place.

She was able to secure Section 8 housing in a brand new high-rise building and asked me to move in with her. I said "Sure, why not." She moved out with my help, and we began to live together. We lived together for about two years before we got married. Unknown to her, I still had about three or four girls on the side working for me, so I couldn't stay home all the time. I had to get out there and do what I do. That created a lot of problems mainly because she had become pregnant. However, I still had to do what I do because I was still the man. I said to myself if she didn't like it, I would leave and let my women take care of me. However, I didn't leave, because I did love her and the kids, but I had to do what I had to do.

One morning my wife had an encounter with Jesus, and that started a whole lot of new problems for me. She put up with me for a long time, and then either she put me out or I left. I was completely strung out on the drugs by then. But she didn't give up on me. She allowed me to come back home. Sometimes I would hear her and the kids praying for me. I thank God for a praying wife. I really gave them a hard way to go. I became president of the IWW Club, the "I Won't Work Club." I was making good money doing my trade and wouldn't work. Plus, I was always strung out on something. When I would run out of money I would guilt her into giving me some. No matter how bad I treated her, she loved me. But I was simply lost. I even had girls working for me a couple of floors below where we lived. That's how lost I was. There were some terrible things that took place, but I don't want to give the enemy any foothold by dredging up all my deeds. But I will say I thank God for saving my wife first.

For years I would watch as she took the bus to church with all the kids. Nothing would stop her. Then, she began ministering at churches, on street corners, revivals, you name it, and she took the children with her. Sometimes I would accompany her, but she was totally sold out to Jesus. One year she told me we were going to move into a house. Yeah, right! We lived in Section 8 housing, I didn't work, and her job was just enough to keep food on the table. We were moving into a house? She began to do some really weird stuff by bringing home pieces of furniture, rugs, and beds and stacking them on our balcony. Between the elements and the pigeons, I just thought she had lost it until one day she told me we needed to go close on our new house. Now that really bugged me. She kept saying that she had prayed and asked the Lord for a house, and here we were getting ready to move into our own home.

Once we moved into the house, my wife opened it up to the children in our new neighborhood to come for Bible study. I thought she had lost her mind. She had fifty or sixty kids in our house at one time! She had recruited a couple of her prayer warriors to come in once a week to teach them about Jesus. It was a bit much for me. But I wasn't around a lot anyway. I had new territory to build. I must admit, I saw some really amazing things take place though. We had Officer Friendly coming to our house. Of course, I knew to stay away when he came through, but after meeting him I kind of liked the guy. Of course, he didn't know what I was up to.

I remember when my wife took me to a cookout she was having. I could not believe what I saw; people were getting baptized in their street clothes! I had never seen anything like it! She didn't have anywhere near enough food for all those people, but we actually carried home several bags of food afterward, not to mention how it had rained so bad. I was sure the event was off. However, it was a gorgeous day. I even sobered up enough to help cook some of the food. My wife would have homeless people staying at our house, feeding them our food and I didn't like it! But everyone loved her. I was the thorn in her side.

Then one night I came home a little spent but on a mission to talk to my daughter about boys. Yes, it was one o'clock in the morning, but I just had to warn her about boys because she was growing up and my wife had all these people in our house. However, before I could finish my conversation, my wife came in. I told her to go to bed, but she wasn't having it. She ordered me out of my daughter's room. I could tell that she was quite upset, but I was too high and just went to bed.

The next day everyone got up, the kids went to school, and my wife went to work, or so I thought. I had stepped out, and when I came home for dinner, no one was home. I waited and waited. Neither the kids nor my wife were around. It began to get late, and they still were not home, so I began asking the neighbors if they had seen them. Nothing. Then it dawned on me that her ex must have done something to them. So, I went to the police station to report them missing. However, they wound up arresting me! They explained that my wife and daughter were afraid that I was attempting to do something terrible to my daughter. Were they out of their minds? I loved my daughter! She may not have been my biological daughter, but she was still mine. I couldn't wrap my head around this. Why would my wife say such a thing! She knew I wouldn't do such a thing.

Well, whatever they said I did, I was not locked up for long. What I would later find out was the fact that my wife was a bit alarmed at my actions toward my daughter. I wanted nothing more than to explain to her what she should not allow boys to do to her. I wanted to warn her about men who would try to take advantage of her. My wife had spoken with the detective and convinced him that I would never do anything to harm my children. She later told me that she asked him to have mercy on me and not allow me to be charged as a felon. The Lord, as always, answered prayers because what I did get was supervised probation and enforced drug-addiction treatment and counseling. The terrible thing about it all was that I could not return home. That was the part that stung the most. What in the world had happened? The devil began to play with my mind, and I became very bitter toward my daughter, thinking that she must have lied on me or something. It just didn't turn out right at all.

Well, as a result, I was out of the house. I found an apartment in uptown DC and thought I had it going on. I didn't need them. As far as I knew, they had all lied on me and almost got me locked up. So, I jumped back into my old trade. I even became friends with the very cops that were supposed to be watching me. For three years it was great being single. But things began to go bad quickly. I had become my own slave again. Nadine would come and visit me sometimes and pray for me and take me to church. I was really broken down. She fed me and then told me I needed to stop what I was doing, straighten up, and come home. Well, once again, the prayers worked. The Lord had mercy on me, and I got my family back.

I went home and really tried not to do drugs. I tried to hang with my wife and her so-called Christian friends. They met every Wednesday evening at the house for a prayer meeting. However, the pull was too strong, and I started the drugs again. I really did try to live a better life. But when I started drugs again, I would try to tempt some of the guys that came by to smoke weed with me. Anyone who would take a hit could not go back into my house to fellowship with my wife and the other saints. I thought they were like my uncle who faked religion. I remember this one guy named Ernie. He was strong in his faith. He wasn't a fake. He was not afraid of me, like the rest of the saints. He was a real man of God and continued to tell me that one day I would change, and until that day he'd pray for me. Between him and my wife, I was listening but not believing.

Then, the joints in my body began to ache really bad, and I needed medical help. The drugs that I had been on had dried up all the fluid in my joints. It was so painful, I could hardly walk. I had to go to the doctor to get steroid shots in the morning and in the evening. This went on for about a few weeks, or maybe months—I don't know because I was still strung out on drugs. I would be downstairs in my house at three and four o'clock in the morning smoking cigarettes and weed and snorting cocaine. My joints hurt so bad that I had to walk with a cane.

One of those nights while sitting downstairs I heard a small voice say to me, "Do you want to be healed?" I thought it was my wife pestering me with her Christian talk. Then that small voice inside of me said, "Just say yes." I heard the voice again say, "Do you want to be healed"? I said nothing again. Then I remembered something from a long time ago. I had read something in the Bible about Samuel hearing a voice speaking to him. I wondered if the Lord could be talking to me. I said to myself, "The next time that voice speaks to me, I'm going to say yes just to see if it is the Lord." I began to remember a long, long time ago when the Lord and I were friends and he had helped me during the time when I was blind and I first got my sight. I remembered other times that I'd gotten in trouble and He would get me out. So when I heard this voice again, I said yes. I thank God that I did. That was the answer that changed my life. I got up to go to the trash can and realized I was walking without my cane. The pains in my joints were completely gone! I went over, took out my brand-new carton of cigarettes and the weed I had stashed away, and began putting them into the trash can. I then went to the sink and got cups of water and began pouring it on the top of my weed, cocaine, and cigarettes.

It seemed like I was walking in a trance because right then at that moment my heart changed. My heart changed, and I felt like a different person. I felt so very sorry for everything I had ever done. Then I began praising the Lord. I went upstairs to tell my wife the good news, but what I saw really got to me. She was already shouting, "Hallelujah, hallelujah, hallelujah!" before I even got upstairs. When I got up there, she said, "I know, baby, I know. She had been upstairs praying for God to save my soul. We both cried and praised the Lord. That was my first encounter with the Lord. Since that day we have been praising and serving the Lord together and will for many, many more years. Praise the Lord!

That's the day the devil's son name left me, and I began to fight against the evil forces that were attempting to destroy my life. Jesus showed up and delivered me. I was baptized as a kid, but this time I received my baptism as a man, and I realized who I was in Christ. The first thing I did was to confess my sin and ask everyone I had mistreated in some way to forgive me. I asked those I knew and the ones I didn't know. I gave up my presidency of the IWW Club. I started a new club called IWFG which means "I Work for God." As a servant of the Lord, He continually showed me the difference between being meek and being weak. As a soldier in the army of the Lord, I learned to fight the good fight of faith. Not fleshly war but spiritual warfare. In the earthly world, they have no witnesses, but in the spiritual world, we become witnesses, witnesses for Christ Jesus. It's called a testimony.

Once the word got out that I was saved, friends came from miles around to see it. No one believed I would ever be saved. I remember a time when some friends traveled to DC from as far as Ohio and Pennsylvania. They had to see this for themselves. They came, they saw, and they believed.

By the time I turned my life over to the Lord, my wife had been in ministry for about twelve or thirteen years. She was an ordained minister of the gospel and a prayer warrior like my sister. I have been walking with the Lord now for over twenty-five years. The first five, He restored my memory and got me a job working for the federal government. I went back to school and got a couple degrees, and then He took me off SSI disability. I started working as a mail clerk, and in less than seven years, I was writing federal disability programs for the government that are still in effect today. He promoted me time and time again, giving me authority over millions of US government programs. But while He was promoting me in the workplace, He was also pouring His word into me. My wife purchased the Bible on video tapes for me, and I would spend hours listening and learning the Word of God. I was being discipled by two pastors and one bishop. I ultimately joined Jericho with my wife and daughter.

Then, I began discipling men myself. I have been discipling men now for over twenty years. My wife and I serve together now, mentoring men and women to follow Jesus. Our calling is to lead people to Christ through the Word of God and by sharing our testimony. God is good, and His faithfulness endures forever. Today, the Lord gives me His word every day to share with everyone I know, in the hopes none would be lost.

There is so much more that I could tell you of how the Lord revealed himself to us as real, time and time again. More recently, our youngest son, who lives in Virginia, was hospitalized with uncontrollable seizures. His wife called us to say she had found him on the floor of his apartment unconscious but twitching. The doctors were trying everything, but nothing would stop the seizures. Our daughter, who is also now a minister of the gospel, went to the hospital and reported that my son was having back-to-back seizures that they could not seem to control. He was unconscious and having seizures. My wife called her Moms in Prayer group and began to wage spiritual warfare on her knees. I could hear her upstairs praying as I was downstairs meeting with our pastor. He was concerned that something was wrong with her, but I told him that is how she would pray for me.

By the time we got to the hospital in Virginia, our son had not had another seizure. While we were driving to the hospital, our daughter called to say he was awake and singing "What a Wonderful World." When we did get to the hospital, we all gathered around his bed and praised God. My wife then told him what had happened to him, because he had no clue. Then my daughter told him that she had to pled the blood of Jesus for his life. My wife had instructed our daughter to whisper in our son's ear and command those spirits to come out of him. When she did, my son went into cardiac arrest, and they had to put everyone out of his room. My daughter called to tell us what had happened, and we bombarded heaven for His life. My daughter was somewhat concerned that she couldn't be with him, but my wife told her walls could not stop the power of God. She told her to continue commanding those spirits to leave as my wife did the same. When our daughter called back with the update, she reported that while the doctors were attempting to put a tube down his throat, he coughed up something. After that he slept like a baby and had no more seizures, none! However, when we got to the hospital and were able to tell him what happened, he began to weep violently. My wife explained to him that the enemy was trying to take his life, but God said, "Not so!"

My son was set apart to God at birth. When he was only two years old, he would pray for and heal people. Once he became an adult, the world snatched him up. He was gifted with a beautiful voice, and the world wanted it. They lured him into shows and fine places, and he stepped away from the Lord. However, my wife and I knew that the Lord was able to keep that which we had committed to him for safekeeping. It was only a matter of time. That morning, our son and his wife rededicated their lives to the Lord, and it has been blessing after blessing as the Lord raised him up from his deathbed.

Nothing and no one can tell us that God is not real. He is very real and very much in control. Oftentimes when things go wrong, we want to blame God. How quickly we forget that there is another guy out there wreaking havoc in the lives of men. His name is Satan. He is the thief that comes to steal, kill, and destroy. God has set the date for his demise, but until then, He has given us power over our enemy! But the sad truth is that people are being destroyed for their lack of knowledge of the Truth. God's Word is Truth.

We are convinced of God's love for His children and His ability to turn their lives around no matter what they have done. This book is a testimony to that fact. I am so very happy the Lord put it on my wife's heart to write this book. It may be that our great-great-grandchildren will need to hear this. There are countless others who will have to go through the great tribulation that God has promised is about to take place. That is when He will remove His people and His Holy Spirit from the world, and Satan will be given the freedom to deceive and destroy many. One of those living during that time may pick up this book and read how God took two very wicked and foolish people and proved to them beyond a shadow of a doubt that He is God and there is none beside Him. We have many, many more testimonies that confirm God is real.

While I was writing my testimony, the Holy Spirit gave me this scripture to share with you. It is written in His Word in the letter to the Ephesians, chapter 4, verse 11–16 (NLT):

> These are the gifts Christ gave to the church: (us) the apostles, the prophets, the evangelists, and the pastors and teachers. Their responsibility is to equip God's people to do His work and build up the church, the body of Christ. This will continue until we all come to such unity in our faith and knowledge of God's Son that we will be mature in the Lord, measuring up to

the full and complete standard of Christ. Then we will no longer be immature like children. We won't be tossed and blown about by every wind of new teaching. We will not be influenced when people try to trick us with lies so clever they sound like the truth. Instead, we will speak the truth in love, growing in every way more and more like Christ, who is the head of His body, the church. He makes the whole body fit together perfectly. As each part does its own special work, it helps the other parts grow, so that the whole body is healthy and growing and full of love.

To God be all the glory forever and ever, amen.

8

A WORD TO THE LADIES

To the lady chosen by God…

—2 John 1:1a (NIV)

Have you ever given much thought to why God the Father chose woman as the medium for all human life that would enter into the realm of this world? No child, male or female, enters into this world without coming through a woman. Do you think God did that as a deliberate act of His Sovereign Will? God, Who does anything He pleases, determined that woman would be the gateway He provided for all human life on this planet! He entrusted us, ladies, with that specific role and responsibility, intending that we, as His daughters, would teach and guide every single life we bring forth into the world to know Who God is and train them to walk in righteousness. We are supposed to be that conduit of God that brings forth His righteous seed into the world, seed that would ultimately crush the head of the enemy of all mankind, Satan. God told Satan after he deceived Eve that "…Because you've done this, you're cursed, cursed beyond all cattle and wild animals, Cursed to slink on your belly and eat dirt all your life. I'm declaring war between you and the Woman, between your offspring and hers. He'll wound your head, you'll wound his heel." (Gen. 3:14–15 MSG).

It is my firm belief that the woman God created in the Garden of Eden was given great ability and played a key role in helping to establish the kingdom of God here on earth. I believe that He gave Eve a role alongside Adam to subdue and conquer the earth as His children. However, our Father's plan was temporarily interrupted by His ancient enemy, Satan. This creature of subtle deception engaged the woman of God in a seemingly simple conversation. However, that conversation was a malignant lie designed to lure her away from the truth. He tricked her into assisting him in his plot to defy the clearly expressed and spoken instructions of her God. Her willingness to entertain Satan's conversation ultimately cost every man and woman on this planet to be separated from the Creator from the moment he or she enters this world. Satan took advantage of Eve by drawing her focus and attention away from her place of dominion beside her husband and caused her to focus on him through his deceptive conversation. She considered Satan's lies as the truth. Ladies, it is no fluke that the same things he offered to Eve he also offered to her offspring, Jesus. They are the same three things he tempts everyone with: the lust and sensual cravings of our flesh, the lust and longing for things we see, and the boastful pride of life: the confidence in our own achievements and possessions. None of those things come from the Father but are from the world as described in 1 John 2:16–17.

The sad truth, my sisters, is that Satan continues this deadly conversation with us today. There is a diabolical plot to attempt to overthrow the kingdom of God. The truth is that it won't happen because "the kingdoms of this world are become the kingdoms of our Lord and His Christ and He shall reign forever and ever!" (Rev. 11:15 KJV).

The deception and distractions must stop, ladies! We must no longer continue to allow our enemy to trick us into doing his bidding, falsely believing that it will lead to our personal satisfaction or happiness. We have an opportunity to follow the example of the God fearing women of the Bible. They no doubt read and understood that the war God declared in the garden would be waged as God said, between them and Satan, and between his children and hers. Consider our sisters Jael (Judg. 4:22-24,

5:24-27), Deborah (Judg. 4), Rahab (Josh. 2), Abigail (1 Sam. 25:1–42), and the mother of our Lord (Luke 1). So many matriarchs of faith that waged war against Satan and came out victorious! Their stories should inspire and stir us to become women of great faith and influence in our world today! May we become the helpmates God designed us to be so that the kingdom of God can be advanced in the earth.

The men of God, and especially our children, need us to return to our rightful place in God's eternal plan. We must not allow the lies of the enemy nor the lures of this world to hinder our purpose and call from God to be the helpers of humankind that He created us to be.

These pages are written to assure you that not only does God love you, but He has victory written into your journey. I want my story to provide the evidence that although Adam and Eve failed to fulfill their God-appointed purpose, it did not stop the Father from going after them and providing for them just the same. He wants to do the same for you! In spite of Eve's sin of entertaining Satan's conversation to the point of defying God, He still vindicated her by sending His Son, the promised seed, born of a woman, to crush Satan's head! Yes, He still used that same woman that failed in the garden to bring about the enemy's demise. That seed born of a woman is Jesus! The Son of the living God Who lives and reigns forever!

The Lord still wants to use His daughters today. However, that can't happen until we surrender to Him so that He can transform us into the newly created women He desires we become as written in Romans 2 Cor. 5:17. The Lord is always ready to raise up another woman of faith who will trust Him. In my lifetime I saw one woman deceived by Satan to convince our government to take all prayer out of America's schools. However, I have also seen God raise up yet another powerful woman of faith to ignite a passion for prayer among women who would take the responsibility of praying over their children and their schools. The welfare of our children must be taken out of the government's hand and put where it should be, in the hands of His daughters! I salute Moms in Prayer International, which began with that one little woman's heart for prayer that has kindled a passion of prayer for children and their schools in over 144 countries. I also applaud them in testimony to my mother, whose prayers moved The Lord's heart to come after me.

I pray that the Lord will reveal His love and truth through my testimony so that it inspires women to respond to Him as Mary, the mother of our Savior did by saying, "Lord, according to Thy Word— so be it unto me!" (Luke 1:38). Are you willing to say that to the Lord? God has counted us worthy to partake of His glory as His daughters. May my story provide evidence for you and inspire you to respond to the call of God upon your life to fulfill His purpose in the earth.

Beloved, read the passage below and then complete this small personal exercise and write your name in the spaces provided. When done, read it aloud to yourself. Then, adopt this statement as true concerning who you are.

But now thus saith the Lord
Who created thee, _____,
and He that formed thee, _____,
Fear not; For I have redeemed thee,
I have called thee by thy name;
THOU ART MINE!

I pray that my testimony may somehow stir your heart to follow Jesus. I also encourage you to ask Him to help you seek out a Titus 2 woman of faith to disciple you. A Titus 2 woman is a mature woman of faith who teaches younger women how to walk out their faith (Titus 2:3-5). I am not saying that men cannot disciple women, especially in group settings. I would however, recommend sex-based one-on-one discipleships. What I am saying is that because it is the last days and many false prophets and lying spirits have been prophesied to come, we must stick to what is clearly written in Titus 2 when Paul specifically instructed Timothy to have the older (not necessarily aged women, but in particular spiritually mature) women teach the younger women sound doctrine. By doing so we minimize the opportunity for Satan to take advantage and get us off course. There are many Christians, such as I was, who foolishly believe they cannot be tempted into sexual sin. As in my case, that is a dangerous and foolish notion. We must always depend and rely upon none other than Jesus Christ to help us overcome the temptations of this world. If it doesn't take much for us to get angry, it won't take much for us to fall into sexual sin.

I will close out this testimony with a revelation the Lord provided me one day. He revealed that before I am a woman, a wife, a mother, a friend, etc., I am first and foremost His child! The differing roles and assignments given to me must not define me. It is what God says about who I am that defines me. He went on to reveal that when humanity was created, God had planned to have an earthly replica or representation of His heavenly kingdom family. "Thy kingdom come, Thy will be done on earth as it is in heaven" bears witness to that plan. The unity, order, and power manifested in the triune godhead would also be manifest in the earthly realm through His creation of Adam, Eve, and their subsequent offspring. This is a great mystery, but I believe that the man, Adam, would represent the head of his family, just as God the Father is the head of the triune family. Jesus Christ, the Son of God, represents God's offspring. Scripture describes Him as "the fullness of the godhead bodily," in Colossians 2:9. However, there are three in the godhead, God the Father, God the Son, and God the Holy Spirit. Jesus Christ possesses the essence of both God the Father and God the Holy Spirit. Similarly, humanity's offspring also possess the essence of both their fathers and their mothers. Please note that I don't indicate that the Holy Spirit is the mother of Jesus Christ. I speak to the similarities in function only. I have relegated it to being a great mystery, just as Jesus suggested in Ephesians 5:31–32 that marriage is a mystery.

However, consider this mystery and correlation between the structure and organization of God's heavenly family: God the Father, God the Son, God the Holy Spirit. Scripture confirms the first Adam became a living being; the last Adam (Jesus) became a life-giving Spirit (1 Cor. 15:45–47). Of the heavenly triune family, God the Holy Spirit provided a relative function or role served by one of Adam's family members, namely the one named Woman, or Eve. I dare not suggest that God, the Holy Spirit is female! Please keep their roles and function at the forefront of your thinking. Believe me, this revelation was as mysterious to me as the purpose of marriage and its heavenly symbol.

As I looked more into Eve's representation, I learned her name means "life spring." According to Adam, she was the mother of all living. Amazingly enough, the word of God also confirms that third person of the godhead—the Holy Spirit "giveth life" (2 Cor. 3:6b KJV).

Certainly, when creation was being fashioned, there had to be a means for bringing forth life on the planet after the creation of Adam and Eve. The vessel God chose as the means for bringing forth new life into this realm was Eve. No human being can enter this realm without coming through the one who brings forth new life—Woman.

Ladies, this is not an issue for personal pride. This is not an opportunity to gloat, usurp, or misinterpret the purpose for which God created woman. We were created alongside the headship He assigned to us, man. If anything, may this revelation lend itself to edify, exhort, and uplift us in our role as the human version, set in the earthly realm, that is somewhat of a similar representation of the presence and power of the Almighty Father, the Holy Spirit.

According to scripture, God created woman as the helpmate for Adam. Concurrently, the Holy Spirit is called *Paraclete* (Gr. παράκλητος, Lat. *paracletus*) which means "advocate or helper." The term *paraclete* most commonly refers to the Holy Spirit, or the One coming alongside to help.

At the same time God was creating an earthly replica of His heavenly family, Satan was plotting to try and disrupt God's plan, knowing exactly where to start. Being one of the wisest and most subtle of God's creatures, he no doubt figured out God's clever design for this triune family, especially the one called woman. I believe he knew of the power and influence that rested upon Eve. He understood the power and influence God had endowed upon this woman and its impact on man.

As the story goes, woman was deceived by Satan and took Adam off course. She desired what Satan offered her more than what God provided for her.

Ladies, please consider the influence God has invested in you. Understand and please wait for the man sent by God to cover you. Don't allow the enemy to draw you away as he did Eve. This culture we now live in teaches women to go after men. However, that is not God's way. This culture teaches women to dress as provocatively as their TV and magazine counterparts portray, suggesting women use their feminine beauty to lure men unto themselves. That is not God's way.

I believe in my heart that I will have to give an account to God for every man that I lured to sin with me. I ignorantly believed the devil's lie and took on his seductive ways to secure what I wanted from men. Although I have repented, the pain of what I may have caused by my prideful, selfish actions still grieves me. Our beauty was not given to us to lure men or establish ourselves as world-made divas. As with Esther, God uses the beauty of His daughters to bring deliverance to the lost. It is given for God's glory and not our own. Beloved, you are precious to the Father. He wrote in His Word that "kings' daughters are among the honorable women. Hearken, O daughter, and consider, and incline thine ear; forget also thine own people (of the world), and thy father's (earthly) house; so shall the (heavenly) king greatly desire thy beauty; for He is the Lord; worship Him!" (Ps. 45:9–11, paraphrased). Keep yourself pure, and be patient. Find a mature woman of faith to walk alongside you and guide you. Read the book of Ruth. She is one of the two women with a chapter in the bible. Get a practical view of what God desires for a female relationships. Paul spoke of it in Titus 2 when instructing Timothy on discipleship in the church that the older women should teach the younger women.

God punished Adam, not so much for eating the fruit as He did for listening to his wife (Gen. 3:17). Like the Holy Spirit, our job as women is to point men in God's direction. Unfortunately, we want men pointed in our direction. We often think we know it all and have one up on the guys intellectually and can tell them a thing or two.

But ladies, that's the lie that initiated the fall in the garden. We are only an extension of what dwells in us. If we are full of ourselves, men don't have much coming. However, if we become the extension of the indwelling Holy Spirit, we will do humankind well.

Now, let's flip the script a bit and imagine where humankind would be today had woman, the most influential creature known to humanity, upheld "the Spirit of Truth." What would have happened if Eve would have upheld the Word of Truth provided by God and resisted the devil, who is the father of lies? (John 8:44). It's probably too hard to imagine.

Ladies—we must not perpetuate this ongoing saga of deception, distraction, and in many cases outright disobedience to our calling. We must stay in step with the Spirit of God so that we may represent Him well in the earthly realm.

The Holy Spirit is invisible—but when He comes into our lives, we know something has happened. Our entire attitude and nature is affected. We begin to witness a transformation in our lives. Women have a similar effect upon our husbands and our homes. We've often heard the saying, when mama's not happy, nobody is happy, or happy wife, happy life. We know what that means. We set the tone for the atmosphere in our homes and elsewhere. We can transform a cold house into a warm home. We can also make it quite unbearable and cause our family to want to run to a corner on the roof rather than face our powerful indignation. The preacher Solomon says it's better to dwell in a corner of the housetop than with a brawling woman in a wide house. (Prov. 25:24).

The love, unity, and synergy that exist between the godhead must also exist in our homes. There should be full cooperation and respect for our husbands, as God has appointed them as His represented head in the home. If we say we submit to God, it should be reflective of our submission and respect for His representative in our homes, our husbands. As we can't begin to imagine all that goes on in the mind of God, we need not expect to grasp all that goes on in the minds of our husbands. Whatever God has endowed them with, one thing is for sure, they are endowed to lead and guide our families. Combined with the endowed inspiration the Father provides through us as willing and cooperative vessels of God, our men would have the needed support and confirmation to lead our families with joy. As we get in step with the Holy Spirit, the true order, love, and power that is provided through the godhead in heaven will be made manifest in our homes here on earth.

Strong's Exhaustive Concordance and Lexicon provides the following concerning the Holy Spirit (wind, air, breath, courage, mind). Their translation of the Hebrew word, *Spirit*, as mentioned in Genesis 1:2 is:

Spirit: rü'·akh (Key)

- *ruwach* (pronunciation)
- Part of Speech: It is a **Feminine noun**

This really caught my eye! The word *Spirit* in Genesis 1:2 is a feminine noun? Well, this find was the icing on the cake for me and caused me to look deeper into my role on earth as woman. The triune godhead has the essence of his feminine creation linked to the role and work of the Holy Spirit. The lights began to come on in my mind and in my heart as the Holy One went on to reveal just how important His daughters are to His eternal plan! We were designed to play an integral role in His earthly replica of the heavenly family. We are valued, vital, and very precious to our Lord.

I could go on, but the main goal of my sharing this revelation is to convince you of what God the Father has created in us as women. One of the key scriptures concerning the Holy Spirit is this: "The Spirit itself *maketh intercession*." That is the revelation that speaks volumes to how important it is that we women keep on praying and teach other women to do the same. As Titus 2 admonishes us, the mature women are to teach the younger women.

I was given the opportunity to share this vision with a group of women that I have come to love and admire greatly. I shared this with the North Carolina chapter of Moms in Prayer International. I discovered this great organization as the result of a prayer to God to help me find a group of women who are faithful and committed to intercessory prayer. I continue to serve alongside women in over 144 countries who take one hour out of their week to come together and touch and agree in prayer for their children and schools. I have been praying with them since 2013, and they do not cease in their commitment and mission to impact lives for Christ by calling women to pray.

Beloved, I am thoroughly convinced that Satan has drawn women away from their key role as intercessors for humankind. The Bible says prayer should go on without ceasing, meaning praying at all times. The unfortunate thing is that we don't have time to pray for our own, much less anyone else. May God have mercy on us!

As women of God, we are vital to humankind's destiny. God has a plan and purpose for every one of us.

As the Holy Spirit teaches—Women, teach your children and other women about the Lord.

As the Holy Spirit Inspires—Women of God, inspire your husbands, your children, and humankind to be all that God designed them to be.

As the Holy Spirit Comforts—Women of God, we are natural-born comforters of crying babies, bruised egos, the aged, and the hurting. That's what we do.

As the Holy Spirit is the Spirit of Truth—Women of God, we must not gossip but speak the Truth in Love.

As the Holy Spirit only speaks what He hears—Women of God, let us speak the Truth as written in God's Word.

Finally, I encourage you to establish a deep and lasting relationship with the Father through His Son, Jesus Christ. May you come to know that you are not in this world without hope or remedy to the situations of life. I pray that you learn that hope must exclusively rest in Jesus Christ, the Son of the living God! He is the only one that can turn your life around.

Today, we live in a culture that has totally forgotten about God. Daily people enter into their routines totally oblivious to His presence and His divine providence over their lives. They also have no idea that we are in the last days, and that sooner than we can imagine, God's judgment is going to come upon all who have not believed in His Son whom He sent with the express purpose of saving us from that judgment!

> For God so loved the world, that he gave his only Son, that whoever believes in him should not perish but have eternal life. For God did not send his Son into the world to condemn the world, but in order that the world might be saved through him. Whoever believes in him is not condemned, but whoever does not believe is condemned already, because he has not believed in the name of the only Son of God.

> John 3:16–18.

So, beloved, as I come to the end of my story, don't forget about the rivers of difficulty and fires of oppression the Lord saw me through. Please know that He can and will do the same for you. This is His promise to you. "When you go through the deep waters, I will be with you. When you go through rivers of difficulty, you will not drown. When you walk through the fire of oppression, you will not be burned up; the flames will not consume you. For I am the Lord, your God" (Isa. 43:2–3 NLT).

Just trust Him and keep your heart open to hear the voice of the Father when He calls to you. Hebrews 3:15 NLT says "…Today when you hear his voice, don't harden your hearts…" Let today be your day of salvation. If you have already surrendered your life to Christ but have not been able to walk it out in victory, just repent, turn back to Him. He will not refuse you. He promises that "all that the Father giveth me shall come to me; and him that cometh to me I will in no wise cast out" (John 6:37 KJV).

Always remember that what He was able to do for me and my family, He is well able to do for you because He loves all His children and He is not a respecter of persons. It is written, "Then Peter opened his mouth, and said, Of a truth I perceive that God is no respecter of persons: But in every nation he that feareth him, and worketh righteousness, is accepted with him" (Acts 10:34–35 KJV).

DISCLAIMER: If you are married, please do not to attempt to handle your marriage the way I did in this book. You must seek God for His wisdom on how to handle your particular situation. Just avoid my mistakes, and trust God for the outcome. I pray that my story will provide you with enough evidence to know and understand that God is very real and very powerful. He also generously rewards all who will diligently seek Him (Heb. 11:6).

I strongly encourage you to seek discipleship with a mature woman of faith otherwise known as a Titus 2 woman of faith? Paul the apostle instructed Timothy, his young disciple to "...teach the older women to live in a way that honors God. They must not slander others or be heavy drinkers. Instead, they should teach others what is good. These older women must train the younger women to love their husbands and their children, to live wisely and be pure, to work in their homes, to do good, and to be submissive to their husbands. Then they will not bring shame on the word of God" (Titus 2:3–5 NLT).

An older woman need not just mean older in age but also older in Christian experience. She will come alongside you and teach you how to walk out your journey. As I mentioned earlier, to get a glimpse of what a Titus 2 relationship might look like, read the book of Ruth. There you will find how a young woman named Ruth pursued Naomi, who was her mother-in law. Naomi was a God-fearing woman who began a discipleship relationship with Ruth instructing her how to conduct herself as a woman of God. Ask The Lord to lead you to a Titus 2 woman of faith who is a member of a community of Christ following believers and follow her as she follows Christ. God does not intend for us to walk out life's uncertain journey alone. He declares that "two are better than one, because they have a good reward for their labor. For if they fall, the one will lift up his fellow: but woe to him that is alone when he fallen; for he hath not another to help him up" (Eccl. 4:9–10 KJV).

MY PRAYER FOR YOU, BELOVED:

Father God, I ask You to move upon the heart of these readers. Allow your Holy Spirit to cause their eyes to be opened so they may see and their ears to be unstopped so they can hear and know just how much you love them. Allow my story to bear witness to your love for them. As I share how You came after me even when I didn't know you or want anything to do with You, reveal how You found me and revealed Yourself and Your love for me. Help me to explain how You opened my eyes to the unchanging Truth of your Word…how you rescued me from Satan's plot to trick me out of the abundant life You purposed for me, for my husband, and for my children. Lord, help them realize that Satan and his band of demons are very real and that they plot every single day to trick us with their lies so that we will wind up in hell with them, forever burning in torment. May they see how, in spite of my ignorance, You had mercy on me and pursued me, forgave me for my ignorant and sinful actions, and then empowered me to live for You. Help me to share how you taught me to fight for my marriage and my family, on my knees. Turn their heart toward You Father, so that they too may experience the joy of your salvation and the wonderful gifts you provide. Rescue them from Satan's plot to steal, kill, and destroy the abundant and eternal life you have destined for them. In Jesus's name, amen!

Made in the
USA
Columbia, SC